DAVID'S MOTHER

by Bob Randall

D0558208

SAMUEL FRENCH, INC.
45 WEST 25TH STREET   NEW YORK 10010
7623 SUNSET BOULEVARD HOLLYWOOD 90046
LONDON   TORONTO

IMPORTANT BILLING AND CREDIT REQUIREMENTS

All producers of DAVID'S MOTHER *must* give credit to the Author of the Play in all programs distributed in connection with performances of the Play and in all instances in which the title of the Play appears for purposes of advertising, publicizing or otherwise exploiting the Play and/or a production. The name of the Author *must* also appear on a separate line, on which no other name appears, immediately following the title, and *must* appear in size of type not less than fifty percent the size of the title type.

David's Mother was presented by the American Stage Company on January 18, 1991, with the following cast:

SALLY	Leslie Ayvazian
BEA	Christine Farrell
DAVID	Andrew Hubatsek
PHILLIP	Terry Layman
JOHN	Al Mohrmann
SUSAN	Lizabeth Zindel
GLADYS	Gisele Richardson
JUSTINE	Maura Russo

Directed by: Michael Murray

David's Mother was presented by the Cleveland Playhouse on October 30, 1991, with the following cast:

SALLY	Ellen Greene
BEA	Carol Locatell
DAVID	Jamie Harrold
PHILLIP	David Berman
JOHN	Kevin Geer
SUSAN	Kendall Harvey
	Lia Snyder
GLADYS	Pamela Tyson
JUSTINE	Lisa Dove

Directed by: Josephine Abady

David's Mother was presented by The Pasadena Playhouse in association with Theatre Corporation of America in September, 1992. The cast (in order of appearance) was:

SALLY .... Ellen Greene
DAVID .... Karl Maschek
GLADYS .... Peggy Blow
BEA .... Carol Locatell
SUSAN... Leah Remini
PHILLIP .... Vasili Bogazianos
JOHN .... Norman Snow
JUSTINE... Jennifer Blanc

Directed by: Josephine R. Abady
Set Design: David Potts
Lighting Design: Marc B. Weiss
Costume Design: Susan Denison Geller
Sound Design: Jeffrey Montgomerie
Original Music by: Steve Orich
Production Stage Manager: Theresa Bentz
Stage Manager: Diana Blazer

CHARACTERS

SALLY

DAVID

GLADYS

BEA

SUSAN

PHILLIP

JOHN

JUSTINE

TIME & PLACE

The present and the past.

The living room of an apartment on the west side
of New York City.

ACT I

Scene 1

SCENE: The living room of an apartment on the west side
of New York City. Present.

The room is and has been in disorder for years. Downstage
right against the wall, is a desk hidden beneath a
plethora of manuscripts and papers. Center is a couch
and a club chair. A coffee table is littered with
magazines and a large filled ashtray.

On the stage left wall, up one step, is the front door of the
apartment. When the door is ajar, it is possible to see
who is in the hall outside.

Downstage left, facing the audience, is another matching
club chair. A small table, piled high with comic books
sits next to it. In front of the chair, facing it, is a TV
set, a VCR and a collection of video cassettes.

AT RISE: The room is empty. The front door is unlocked
and SALLY enters laden down with grocery bags.
SHE's in her forties and wears an unflattering down
jacket and jeans. Her lack of vanity borders on
sloppiness. SHE puts the groceries down on the coffee
table and crosses to the video cassettes.

SALLY. Alright, David, we are pleased to present, for
our matinee today, the MGM classic, *The Wizard of Oz.*
Starring Judy Garland, Frank Morgan ... (*SHE sees that*

DAVID has not entered the apartment. SHE calls to him.)
Move it, David. The credits have started.

*(DAVID appears in the doorway. He is sixteen years old,
dressed in jeans and a windbreaker. HE is severely
damaged; retarded, possibly more. HE enters the
apartment.)*

SALLY. Close the door.

(HE comes down the step into the living room.)

SALLY. David, close the door.

(HE turns, steps up and closes the door.)

SALLY. Starring Judy Garland, Frank Morgan, Ray
Bolger, Bert Lahr and Jack Haley ...

*(DAVID hurries to the club chair and sits awkwardly,
smiling at the set in anticipation. SALLY puts the
cassette into the VCR and fast forwards.)*

SALLY. ... From the book by L. Frank Baum, lyrics
by E.Y. "Yip" Harburg, music by Harold Arlen, directed by
Victor Fleming, produced by Mervyn Leroy, approximate
screening time one hour forty-one minutes, copyright
Loew's Incorporated. Enjoy.

*(SALLY presses the play button, kisses David on the
forehead and crosses to the groceries. DAVID sits there,*

mesmerized by the film which plays softly in the background.)

SALLY. You want Stouffer's lasagna or Weight Watcher's stuffed cabbage for lunch? If I were you, I'd take the cabbage because I got Lean Cuisine spaghetti and meatballs for dinner. Weight Watcher's it is? This is living! (*SHE imitates Lynn Redgrave's final flourish on the commercial and exits into the kitchen with the groceries.*)

(In a moment, the front DOORBELL rings.)

SALLY. (*Off.*) Wait a minute, I gotta set the microwave! (*In a beat, SALLY enters.*) Shit. Were you expecting somebody? (*SHE crosses to the front door and puts the chain on.*) Who is it?
GLADYS. (*Off.*) It's Gladys Johnson.
SALLY. (*Soto.*) Shit.

(SALLY opens the door a crack on the chain. GLADYS stands there. SHE's in her thirties, black.)

GLADYS. I wonder if you could spare me a minute?
SALLY. Now's a bad time, Miss Johnson. Why don't I give you a call?
GLADYS. It's quite urgent that we speak. I've written to you twice ...
SALLY. Have you? Darn that post office!
GLADYS. I slipped both letters under your door.
SALLY. Oh, *those* letters. Right. Look, Miss Johnson, at the moment, I've got a houseful of guests. (*To an*

imaginary guest.) Yip, try the dip. (*To Gladys.*) I'll give you a call.

GLADYS. I hope you will.

SALLY. Bye. (*SALLY closes the door and crosses to the desk to search for a cigarette.*) The wolves are nipping at our heels, honeybunch. But don't you worry. She's not going to get her hands on you. I promise you that, David. *Nobody fucks with you!* Where's a cigarette? (*SHE finds an empty pack.*) Terrific. I remembered every goddamn kind of pasta made, but I forgot my carcinogens. You're wise not to smoke, David. It's a dirty and degrading habit. Don't worry, one of these days I'm going to clean up this place. I know how disorder offends you.

(*The MICROWAVE timers goes off in the kitchen.*)

SALLY. Coming! Hiya Toto! Don't be a smuck! Leave the cat alone. (*SHE exits into the kitchen. In a beat SHE enters with their lunches on a tray and a bottle of wine. SHE places his lunch in front of him and puts a spoon in his hand.*) Use the spoon, David.

(*SALLY takes her own lunch and the wine to the couch and looks over at DAVID who has started to eat with his fingers.*)

SALLY. David, I'm not playing miracle worker with you. Use the spoon!

(*HE takes more food into his right hand, transfers it to his left and into his mouth.*)

SALLY. David darling, use the spoon. Sweetheart, light of my life, use the spoon ... USE THE SPOON, DAVID!!

(HE picks up the spoon and puts food on it with his fingers. Then HE transfers the spoon to his left hand and into his mouth.)

SALLY. Good boy.

(The DOORBELL rings.)

SALLY. Johnson? Again?

(SALLY hurries to the TV set and turns off the volume. SHE puts her hands over her mouth to indicate to David to be quiet. HE imitates her.)

BEA. *(Off.)* It's too late. I know you're in there. Open up.

SALLY. Crap. *(Loud enough for her to hear.)* David, it's Auntie Bea, come to call. What a treat.

(SALLY opens the door and BEA sweeps into the room past her. Bea is Sally's sister, several years older, smartly dressed.)

SALLY. Sorry, I didn't hear the bell.

BEA. Sure. I should think you'd welcome somebody to talk to.

SALLY. I got somebody to talk to. David and I were just discussing cutlery.

BEA. I heard. So did everybody on the floor. (*BEA crosses to David and kisses him on the top of his head. SHE sees HE is eating with his fingers.*) Everybody except David.

SALLY. Use the spoon, David.

BEA. (*Seriously.*) Sit down. I want to talk to you.

SALLY. Who's dead?

BEA. Abraham Lincoln. Sit down.

(*THEY sit on the couch and wingback chair. BEA sees the wine bottle.*)

BEA. You drink wine in the middle of the day now?

SALLY. It's left over from the Academy Awards. I had a party.

BEA. (*Not believing her.*) Oh yeah? Who'd you invite?

SALLY. Some movie stars you don't know. Joan Caulfield and Turhan Bey. Leave me alone.

BEA. I don't have to leave you alone. I'm your sister.

SALLY. So don't leave me alone. What're you doing so far from Sutton Place, anyway?

BEA. Stephen and I are having a brunch on Sunday. I needed scotch salmon.

SALLY. I'm fresh out.

BEA. And you're coming.

SALLY. Thank you very much but I have a previous engagement.

BEA. What previous engagement?

SALLY. I'll think of something.

BEA. Sally, he's a very nice man.

SALLY. Oh, boy. You don't even try to pretend you're not fixing me up.

BEA. Why should I pretend? I'm your sister.

SALLY. I'm not coming.

BEA. Yes you are. Justine will be here at eleven to watch David. (*To David.*) Your cousin's coming to stay with you, sweetheart. (*SHE sees that DAVID had his hand down the front of his pants.*) He's playing with himself.

SALLY. Don't look.

BEA. Sally, David is playing with himself.

SALLY. So, how much fun does he have? Leave him alone.

BEA. There is right and there is wrong. Even the disabled have to learn the difference. David, darling, don't do that. I mean it. Cut it out.

(*DAVID looks over at her and withdraws his hand.*)

SALLY. (*Impressed.*) Now see if you can get him to eat with a spoon.

BEA. He's very charming.

SALLY. I take it we're not talking about David anymore.

BEA. He's in his forties, a widower, no children.

SALLY. What're you doing? Getting the hundred neediest cases together?

BEA. I told him all about you and David. He'd love to meet you both.

SALLY. We'd love to meet him, too, but I just remembered what we're doing Sunday.

BEA. What?

SALLY. We joined a bridge club.

BEA. You don't play bridge.

SALLY. I'm learning. Besides, David likes it. He gets to be the dummy.

BEA. That's not funny. That's not the least bit funny. What's happening to you?

SALLY. You mean besides my teeth shifting?

BEA. I mean your sense of humor. You're becoming a macabre person, Sally. And a recluse. You turn down every invitation. Well, this is one you're not going to turn down. If you don't show up, we'll come here.

SALLY. I won't open the door.

BEA. I have a key. (*Holding out her hand.*) Give me your hand. (*SALLY obeys.*) You're my sister and I love you.

SALLY. I know that part.

BEA. You've been dealt a rough hand to play ...

SALLY. You mean at the bridge club?

BEA. Stop that.

SALLY. Sorry.

BEA. (*Crossing to David.*) All I want to do is try to make your life better. And you thwart me at every turn.

(*SHE attempts to feed David a spoonful of food. HE wails in protest.*)

BEA. What'd I do?!

SALLY. Only the left hand can put food in his mouth. Don't you know anything?

BEA. Why?!

SALLY. That's a little secret between David and God.

BEA. (*Going back to Sally; DAVID continues to eat with his fingers.*) Where were we?

SALLY. I was thwarting you at every turn.

BEA. I worry about you.

SALLY. You don't have to.

BEA. But I do. I worry and I feel guilty. It could have happened to either of us.

SALLY. Define "it."

BEA. You know what I'm talking about. Eat slower, David.

SALLY. David is not an "it." He's a "he."

BEA. I was talking about his disability. I have two bright children. I can't help it. I feel guilty.

SALLY. Don't. Feel lucky.

BEA. (*Crossing back to David.*) You're coming Sunday and I don't want to hear another word about it.

SALLY. God, you're as bossy as Ma.

BEA. With one difference. I don't enjoy being bossy. (*SHE strokes David's hair.*)

SALLY. You could've fooled me.

BEA. Justine will be here at eleven. Wear something that doesn't have dried food on it.

SALLY. I'll have to go shoplift a new frock. I already expended my expendable income.

BEA. I'll buy you one.

SALLY. No, thanks.

(*DAVID starts to put his hand down the front of his pants again. BEA holds his hand, preventing it.*)

BEA. That's enough of that, David. (*To Sally.*) You want to wear something of mine?

SALLY. No, thanks. I'll wear my old wedding gown. As I recall, I was too nervous to eat while I had it on.

BEA. I'm not picking on you.

SALLY. You could've fooled me twice.

BEA. Sometimes it's the only way to deal with you. You're not an easy person, you know.

SALLY. True.

BEA. Alright, I've got to go. (*SHE kisses David.*) Be a good boy and don't abuse yourself too much. (*To Sally.*) Give me a hug.

(*THEY meet center stage and hug.*)

SALLY. Two old battleships collide.

BEA. (*Beat.*) I got a letter from Susan.

SALLY. Susan who?

BEA. Your daughter Susan, that's Susan who. She's pregnant.

SALLY. She's only nineteen!

BEA. She's twenty.

SALLY. (*Beat, recovering from the surprise.*) Already? Did she happen to mention whether or not she got married?

BEA. They're getting married in a few weeks.

SALLY. That's what I like. First things first.

BEA. Why don't you call her?

SALLY. If she heard from me, she might miscarry. We're not that close, since she chose to move three thousand miles away.

BEA. You should go to her wedding.

SALLY. I don't have the wardrobe.

BEA. So buy the wardrobe.

SALLY. With what? (*Indicating the messy desk.*) I'm a freelance editor, not a writer.

BEA. I'll give you the money.

SALLY. No.

BEA. It would be my pleasure.

SALLY. It was your pleasure to buy us the VCR. I don't like you enough to make you that happy.

BEA. Did I mention you're not an easy person?

SALLY. Somebody did. I suppose it was you.

BEA. Alright, now I'm really going. I'll see you Sunday. Or else.

SALLY. I said okay. Go. I have to start scraping a dress.

(BEA exits. SALLY turns to David.)

SALLY. Did you hear? Your sister is pregnant. And getting married. And twenty. Boy, you and I are out of touch.

(DAVID reacts to the movie with fear. HE hugs SALLY who is sitting on the arm of his chair.)

SALLY. Don't feel bad. Just because you didn't get invited to the wedding. Neither did I. Which is just as well considering that person would be there. You remember him? The one who used to be your father?

(DAVID calms down and pulls away from Sally. HE stares at the TV screen. SALLY starts to clean some dropped food from the floor.)

SALLY. Not that it would have killed her to invite us. I used to be her mother.

SUSAN. (*Off. Her voice is in the past and SALLY doesn't hear it. Or she chooses not to.*) I don't want to talk about it!

PHILLIP. (*Off. Also in the past.*) Come on, Susan. You were fine ...

(*HE opens the front door. SUSAN, in her early teens stomps in petulantly, unseen by SALLY. PHILLIP enters, closes the door and hangs up his coat. SUSAN flops down on the couch disconsolately.*)

SALLY. (*Finishing the floor.*) You want anything else to eat? There's still room on the floor.

PHILLIP. (*Calling out.*) Sally? Sarah Bernhardt and I are home!

SUSAN. Very funny.

SALLY. (*To David.*) Some Oreos?

PHILLIP. (*To Susan.*) Everybody forgets lines ...

SUSAN. Daddy, will you stop?! Will you just forget the goddamn play?!

SALLY. (*Shocked into the past by Susan's language.*) Susan, watch the mouth! What's the matter?

PHILLIP. She's upset. She forgot a few lines in the play.

SALLY. In *Romeo and Juliet*? Who would notice? I bet everybody thought that's the way it was supposed to be.

SUSAN. How would you know? You weren't even there.

SALLY. Susan, the baby sitter cancelled. What was I supposed to do? Bring David? Even *I* fidget at Shakespeare!

SUSAN. Right. Make a joke.

PHILLIP. (*To Susan.*) Honey, nobody's making a joke. Come on, don't be mad at your mother. She didn't write that play. They don't even know if Shakespeare did.

SUSAN. (*Heading for her room.*) I'm glad everybody is having a good time at my expense. (*Exits.*)

PHILLIP. (*Calling after her.*) I thought you were terrific! (*To Sally.*) Did I handle that wrong?

SALLY. Look who you're asking. How would *I* know?

(THEY share a rueful little laugh.)

SALLY. Was she terrific?

PHILLIP. Only compared to Romeo. He had adenoids. (*Exiting into kitchen, speaking with adenoidal voice, gesturing toward the kitchen in a Shakespearean pose.*) But soft, what light from yonder window breaks? ... Is there any meatloaf left?

(SUSAN enters, also heading into the kitchen.)

SALLY. Are you ready to stop sulking now?

SUSAN. No.

SALLY. Susan, it's junior high school. The critics weren't there.

SUSAN. Neither were you.

SALLY. (*Beat.*) Sometimes you're a real little beast, you know that?

SUSAN. (*Said matter-of-factly.*) Yeah, I hate you, too.

SALLY. You don't hate me. I'm your mother. It doesn't work that way. You may resent me, you may be filled with ambivalence, offended and indignant as hell, but trust me, daughters do not hate their mothers. Except in my case, which is different. Now come give me a kiss and cut out this crap.

(SUSAN crosses to her begrudgingly. SALLY presents her cheek. SUSAN gives her a small resentful peck.)

SALLY. That's the best you can do?

(SUSAN gives her another peck.)

SALLY. You want one?
SUSAN. *(Hurries off to the kitchen.)* Some other time.
SALLY. *(Calling after her, half kidding.)* Ooh, you sour little creep. Don't give her any meatloaf! *(SHE returns to the present and David.)* So who cares if we're not going to her wedding? My feelings aren't hurt, are yours? The hell with it. What does she think? We can't behave ourselves in front of her father's fancy friends? She's so afraid I'll say something and you'll act up. *(Lovingly to David.)* As if you can help it. As if you chose to act up. As if you're thinking things we don't know about ... *(SALLY slowly starts to slip into an old fantasy; that David is whole. Her demeanor changes; it becomes dreamlike.)* ... Are you? Are you, David? Are you thinking something I don't know about?

(SHE turns his face to hers. HE smiles, entirely by accident. SHE returns the smile but one filled with pain.)

SALLY. Is it an act, sweetheart? Are you thinking "Fuck you, lady, I'm not going to let on to all I think and all I know?" Is that why you're smiling? Because I'm right? (*SHE holds his head to her breast, kissing the top of it.*) Can you think, you son-of-a-bitch? Can you think and you just don't want me to know? Is that what's going on here? (*SHE rests her head on top of his.*)

(*The LIGHTS dim.*)

Scene 2

Later.
We hear the soundtrack from The Wizard of Oz.
DAVID is stretched out on the couch. HE brings his right
    hand up to his face and wiggles his fingers directly in
    front of his eyes. HE repeats the action with his left
    hand. Back to the right hand as SALLY enters from up
    right carrying several dresses which SHE puts on the
    couch. SHE turns off the sound of the TV.

SALLY. Alright, which little piggy goes to brunch? (*SHE takes David's hands in hers and stops him from wiggling his fingers.*) Enough. There's still ten of them.

(*SHE releases his hands and HE folds them on his mouth.*
    SALLY holds up a dark blue pin-striped dress in front
    of herself and models it for him.)

SALLY. You like? (*Beat, no reaction from DAVID.*) No? You're right. It makes me look like a prison matron. How about this one? (*SHE holds another dress in front of her. DAVID pays no attention.*) David, you're always nagging me to get out and meet people, now help me! (*SHE strikes a model's pose.*) Here we see Sally in a two-piece acrylic creation, equally at home yachting the afternoon away or relaxing in the frozen produce section of the A&P. (*SHE looks down at herself, deflates, drops the dress.*) Do me a favor. Call your aunt and tell her I'm not coming. I don't need this humiliation.

(*The DOORBELL rings.*)

SALLY. Why won't they leave us alone? Coming! (*SHE crosses to the door and puts the chain on.*) Who's there?

GLADYS. (*Off.*) Gladys Johnson.

SALLY. (*Hesitates, suddenly nervous.*) Just a minute! I'm not dressed. (*Hurries DAVID off to his room.*) Play in your room. Count your fingers (*To Gladys.*) Coming! (*SHE crosses to the front door and opens it.*) Sorry I didn't call. My company just left.

GLADYS. (*Entering.*) Thank you for seeing me.

SALLY. That's alright. I've only got a minute, though. (*Indicating dresses.*) My dressmaker's coming over. Sit down.

(*GLADYS sits uncomfortably on the couch. Her demeanor is authoritative but SHE also seems ill-at-ease with the policemanlike position she finds herself in.*)

GLADYS. I think my letters explained everything.

SALLY. (*Lying.*) Which letters were those?

GLADYS. Mrs. Goodman, I'm with the Department of Child Welfare ...

SALLY. Oh, yeah. *Those* letters. Well, Miss Johnson...

GLADYS. *Mrs.* Johnson.

SALLY. Oh, you're married. Isn't that nice?

GLADYS. I'm divorced.

SALLY. (*Trying to charm her out of her determination.*) Me, too. Small world. Sometimes I think marriage has had it. Maybe that's the best way. A relationship's hard enough without a piece of paper to screw it up, don't you think?

GLADYS. I don't know. Mrs. Goodman ...

SALLY. Call me Sally, Gladys.

GLADYS. Sally, as I explained in those letters, they're taking a new census of handicapped minors in the tri-state area and when the Connecticut computers were put on line with New York, a discrepancy was discovered in your son's file.

SALLY. No, really?

GLADYS. New York has him assigned to a facility in Connecticut but Connecticut has never heard of him.

SALLY. Oh. That *is* a discrepancy, isn't it?

GLADYS. Yes. He seems to have slipped through the cracks.

SALLY. How agile of him.

GLADYS. Is he in a program?

SALLY. Oh, please, he's been in a hundred of them. Some were pretty good, too. I have to hand it to you people at the Department of Child Welfare, you know your stuff ...

GLADYS. Is he in one now?

SALLY. Well, not exactly now. He's temporarily between programs.

GLADYS. How long has he been temporarily between programs?

SALLY. Not long.

GLADYS. Let's not play games, Mrs. Goodman. It's a state law that every handicapped minor has to be in a program. Is he in one or not?

(Beat. SALLY hesitates.)

GLADYS. It's not a hard question, Mrs. Goodman. If he's in a program, please tell me. Because if you don't, I'll have to report it.

SALLY. Why?!

GLADYS. Because if I don't, I could lose my job. And I can't afford to lose this job. So, please, be straight with me?

SALLY. *(Giving in.)* What d'you want to know?

GLADYS. *(Consulting her pad.)* The last information we have on David was the Clinton School. Was that his last placement?

SALLY. Yes.

GLADYS. Then where did the authorities get the idea he was going into a program in Connecticut?

SALLY. I guess they got it from me. Because I told them so. I told them we were moving, to a nice little town with a white church and a steeple and a couple of antique shops.

GLADYS. You lied.

SALLY. Don't be scared. It happens.

GLADYS. Why did you do it?

SALLY. Why else? To protect him.

GLADYS. There are other programs.

SALLY. No shit. We've been there. Programs and schools and hospitals and centers for rehab and guidance and therapy and plain babysitting. And all that ever happened was he got the shit scared out of him. My son is damaged. He's not going to wake up one day and say "Wow! I feel better. Send me to college." This is as good as it gets. But it only gets good *here*. Within these four walls in need of painting. *This* is where he's safe. *This* is where he's happy. And *this* is where you've got to let him stay! Please, Gladys! Couldn't you put it in your report that you didn't find us?

GLADYS. (*Beat, sadly.*) I can't do that.

SALLY. (*Angry at Gladys for her refusal and at herself for begging.*) No, of course you can't. You can't change your *rules*. You and the whole medical establishment who think you ate at the last supper. You can't bend. (*Beat, bitterly.*) You enjoy your work, Gladys?

GLADYS. Not always. Mostly I enjoy the paycheck. It *almost* supports my two kids now that their father took off.

SALLY. You too, huh.

GLADYS. Me too.

SALLY. (*Beat, understanding that Gladys is only doing what she has to do, SHE softens.*) Do you think they can smell this planet in the next galaxy?

GLADYS. I wouldn't be at all surprised.

SALLY. How old are your kids?

GLADYS. My daughter's six. Her brother's three.

SALLY. My daughter's three years older than David, too.

GLADYS. It's a good age difference.

SALLY. Not around here it wasn't. Would it do any good to plead with you not to turn us in, one deserted mother to another?

GLADYS. Listen, if it was up to me, I wouldn't even be here. I'd be home with my sick boy.

SALLY. What's he got?

GLADYS. The usual.

SALLY. Try chicken soup with lemon in it. Don't laugh. It works.

GLADYS. (*With a sigh, SHE rises.*) Let's talk again, okay?

SALLY. What're you going to do?

GLADYS. Oh, I guess I'll go kick myself in the butt for putting off what has to be done. David's going into a program, Sally. The sooner you get used to that, the sooner you'll both be happy. Think about it, will you?

SALLY. Do I have a choice?

GLADYS. No.

(*The front door opens as GLADYS crosses to it and SUSAN and PHILLIP enter in the past, unseen. SUSAN rushes in happily, PHILLIP hangs up his coat in the closet.*)

SUSAN. Ma!

SALLY. (*Extending her hand to Gladys.*) Don't think it hasn't been fun.

SUSAN. Ma?! Ma?!

PHILLIP. (*Happily to Susan.*) Take it easy.

(SALLY and GLADYS shake hands. GLADYS exits and SALLY closes the door after her. SUSAN has run into the kitchen in search of her mother and now enters and sees her.)

SUSAN. Ma, we're gong away!

SALLY. *(Turning, in the past now.)* Oh yeah? Where are we going?

SUSAN. To the novelty!

PHILLIP. The Nevele.

SALLY. Yeah? Who died and made us rich?

PHILLIP. All six salesmen and their families are going. So Friedman can take it off his taxes instead of giving us a bonus, but what the hell—*(HE holds out his arms and SUSAN runs into them.)* We're going to eat and swim and eat and play tennis and eat …

SALLY. *(Unmoved.)* We'll talk about it.

PHILLIP. What's to talk about? Friedman is paying.

SALLY. *(Exiting into the bedrooms.)* We'll see.

PHILLIP. *(To Susan.)* Your mother is a downer, you know?

SUSAN. I know.

PHILLIP. Hey, I'm allowed. You're not.

(SALLY enters with DAVID. PHILLIP is shocked to see him. SALLY takes him to his chair by the TV set.)

PHILLIP. What's David doing here? *(Beat.)* Go to your room, Susan. Go.

(SUSAN obeys reluctantly. SALLY turns on the TV for David without sound, aware that a fight is on the way.)

PHILLIP. Who took him out of the home?

SALLY. I took him out of the home.

PHILLIP. (*Bitterly.*) Again.

SALLY. You weren't there. You didn't see.

PHILLIP. I didn't have to. It's always difficult at first. How many times have they told us that?

SALLY. *Difficult?* Yeah, that's a good word. Doctors have a lot of good, clean words that don't mean anything. Like *playroom.* That's another good one. I saw him in the *playroom,* sitting off by himself, staring. No, maybe *cowering* is a better word. Cowering in front of a picture on the wall, not understanding what he did that was so bad that his mommy and daddy sent him to that place ...

PHILLIP. (*Tenderly.*) Sally ...

SALLY. And when I went over to him, you know what? He was all wet. He had peed himself. Yeah, there was my baby sitting there in his own urine in that fucking *playroom* ...

PHILLIP. (*Takes her in his arms.*) You've got to give it time.

SALLY. Time? How much time? How long does he have to suffer? Till he doesn't know who we are? Till he has a stroke?

PHILLIP. (*Comforts her, kissing her forehead.*) We'll keep him for a few days and then we'll try again.

SALLY. I can't.

PHILLIP. Yes, you can. You'll see.

SALLY. (*Pulling out of his embrace.*) I already see. I see that you want him out of your life.

PHILLIP. I want him out of my life? Are you crazy? He's my son!

SALLY. I'm sorry.

PHILLIP. You're not sorry.

SALLY. (*Resenting that.*) Alright, have it your own way. I've got no time to be sorry. I've got a kid to raise. *Your* kid.

PHILLIP. You think you're the only one it happened to? Didn't it happen to me?! Didn't it happen to Susan?!

SALLY. No! You're at your office all day kidding around with the secretaries. Susan is at school playing. I'm the one chained to him! It happened to *me*!

(Upstage, SUSAN is seen in the hallway. Her hands are over her ears, not wanting to hear her parents fight. PHILLIP sees her. HE slams his fist into the couch and exits after her.

SALLY moves to the pile of dresses and back into the present. SHE picks up a dress, holds it in front of herself and struts, model style, for David.)

SALLY. (*Heading for the phone.*) And now, the piece de resistance of the collection, a smashing blend of trevira and orlon ... (*SHE dials.*) A double knit fantasy, an acrylic dream come true, a fashion triumph ... (*Into the phone, deflating.*) Bea? Alright. You can buy me a dress.

(The LIGHTS dim.)

Scene 3

The next day.

*SALLY and DAVID are sitting on the floor on opposite
sides of the coffee table. A Monopoly game is in
progress, but SALLY is playing for both of them.
DAVID sits there, wiggling his fingers in front of his
eyes.*

SALLY. (*Rolling the dice.*) Come on three! ... Five,
damn it. (*Moving her man.*) One, two, three, four, five.
Park Place. I already own it. (*Handing DAVID the dice.*)
Roll a six, baby. That'll put you on Ventnor which is
mine with a hotel. Roll a six. Come on, six.

(DAVID holds the dice but doesn't throw them.)

SALLY. Roll 'em, baby. Six. Come to Mama.

(HE still doesn't roll the dice.)

SALLY. Roll 'em already!

*(DAVID throws the dice on the floor and goes back to
twiddling his fingers. SALLY hurries to the dice.)*

SALLY. Six! You rolled a six! (*SHE hurries back to
the board and takes David's hand in hers, helping him to
move his man.*) One, two, three, four, five, six ... Oh,
look! Ventnor Avenue with a hotel! That'll be eleven
hundred dollars! I'm hot! I'm hot!

(The DOORBELL rings.)

SALLY. *(Suddenly tense, thinking it's Johnson.)* Shit. *(SALLY crosses to the door.)* Who is it?

BEA. *(Off.)* It's me.

SALLY. *(Opens the door, relieved.)* *Now* what?

BEA. What d'you mean, now what? I want to see the dress I bought you. Put it on.

SALLY. Get stuffed.

BEA. *You* get stuffed. Into the dress.

SALLY. Alright, I guess you're entitled to something for six hundred dollars.

BEA. *(Taken back but covering.)* Six hundred? Fine.

SALLY. A hundred and twenty. I had you scared, huh?

BEA. *(Crossing to David.)* Shut up. Hi, David. You're playing Monopoly?

SALLY. He just lost. He rolled a six. To tell you the truth, he rolled a four. Close enough. *(Crossing to the up right exit.)* Put on *E.T.* for him.

BEA. You've got *E.T.*?

SALLY. *(Exiting.)* What do you think this is, a slum?

BEA. You want an answer or an argument? *(BEA finds the cassette and inserts it into the machine.)*

SALLY. *(Off.)* He likes a build up. It whets his appetite for the movie.

BEA. What kind of build up?

SALLY. *(Off.)* You know, now presenting *E.T.*, one of the highest grossing films in motion picture history, directed by Stephen Spielberg, a great cinematic achievement ...

BEA. *(Leading DAVID to his chair.)* I never liked it.

SALLY. (*Off.*) Who asked you? Turn off the sound. He likes looking at it.

BEA. Thank God for small favors. Now presenting *E.T.*, the most overrated puerile film ever made. Starring a stupid looking puppet and saccharine to the point of nausea.

(*BEA turns up the volume and we hear MUSIC. DAVID beams.*
SALLY enters in the dress. It's the first time we see that she's an attractive woman with a good figure.)

SALLY. Ta Ta!

BEA. Now you look like a human being.

BEA. (*Looking at Sally's new dress.*) What are you going to do with your hair?

SALLY. I can't decide between corn rows and dreadlocks.

BEA. I'm going to smack you.

SALLY. You got time to get drunk before you go back to your spic-and-span apartment and eat off the floor?

BEA. What've you got besides that lousy wine you drink?

SALLY. I got some lousy gin. And some flat tonic.

BEA. Who could resist?

(*SALLY exits into the kitchen, up left. BEA crosses to the desk, looks disparagingly at the mess.*)

BEA. Did you ever think of cleaning this space?

SALLY. (*Off.*) Sure. I think about it all the time.

BEA. (*Crossing to the couch.*) Should I send Annie over?

SALLY. (*Off.*) No.

BEA. Why not?

SALLY. (*Off.*) It would give you too much pleasure.

BEA. David, your mother is a slob. (*Off, to Sally.*) At the risk of pressing my luck, can I treat you to the beauty parlor?

SALLY. (*Off.*) Shut up already about the way I look.

BEA. I'm your sister.

SALLY. (*Entering with their drinks.*) You're subverting my self image.

BEA. What self image?

SALLY. I have a strong self image. Me and the cookie monster share one. (*Handing BEA her drink.*) Here, choke.

(*BEA sits on the couch, SALLY in the wingback chair.*)

BEA. I'm sorry. I just believe in putting your best foot forward.

SALLY. Bea, this *is* my best foot. Before you turn me into an after, what's he like?

BEA. Not bad.

SALLY. That bad, huh?

BEA. I say not bad so you say bad. Black.

SALLY. He's black?

BEA. No, I just wanted to hear you say white. (*BEA kicks off her shoes and tucks her feet up under her.*)

SALLY. Don't get too comfortable. You're staring to irritate me.

BEA. Unlike everything else in the world, huh?

SALLY. You think? Am I really that hard to get along with?

BEA. Not compared to some.

SALLY. Like who?

BEA. Joseph Goebbles, Joan Crawford, our mother.

SALLY. Yes, I've turned into some piece of work.

BEA. Hey, I'm kidding.

SALLY. Hey, I'm not.

BEA. What's the matter with you? You're the one who's always right, remember?

SALLY. Yeah, only as the years go by and I look around at the growing hordes of those who are always wrong, I wonder.

BEA. Stop wondering. You're the best.

SALLY. Yesterday in the supermarket, there was this little girl about seven. She kept staring at David. Wherever we went, there she was, staring at him. I hated that little girl. I actually hated her.

BEA. That's only natural.

SALLY. It's not natural to hate a little kid. I should have said "Sweetheart, it's not nice to stare."

BEA. What did you say?

SALLY. "Quit staring. You're not so pretty yourself." The worst thing is she wasn't pretty. What kind of person tells a homely kid she isn't pretty?

BEA. Someone who's tired.

SALLY. I can't afford to be tired. (*Beat.*) So, what's he like?

BEA. Cute.

SALLY. Then why'd you say not bad?

BEA. Because if I said he was cute you wouldn't come.

SALLY. (*Worried.*) How cute?

BEA. Depends on your perspective. I like chubby men. His name is Marvin …

SALLY. Marvin? You're fixing me up with a Marvin?

BEA. Marvin Bernstein. I think he's Jewish but I might be wrong.

SALLY. What does he do?

BEA. He's retired.

SALLY. Before he got too infirm to work, what did he do?

BEA. (*Stifling a laugh.*) He was a chiropractor.

SALLY. You're so full of shit, Bea.

(BEA laughs out loud, feeling the gin. SALLY is amused.)

SALLY. The truth, please.

BEA. His name is John Patrick Nicklaus. He owns a couple of big wallpaper and paint stores. He's been a widower for over a year. He's such a sweet guy and he's so lonely.

SALLY. Swell. Get 'em while they're down, huh? I'm surprised you didn't invite me to his wife's funeral.

BEA. Stephen wouldn't let me. (*SHE laughs again.*) I don't drink in the afternoon.

SALLY. No shit. I hope you didn't get too much smoked salmon, because I'm not coming.

BEA. Stop being so insecure. You're a very attractive woman.

SALLY. Damn right.

BEA. Besides, at our age, what do looks have to do with anything?

SALLY. What does that mean? I'm not a very attractive woman? Moron.

(DAVID reacts to the movie, upset, pointing and moaning.)

SALLY. Alright, I'm coming. *(SHE crosses to the VCR and fast forwards.)* He doesn't like that scene. *(SHE presses play.)* There, the bad part's gone. *(Returning to Bea.)* Go home. I gotta turn shit into literature.

BEA. *(Getting up.)* Alright. *(SHE puts her shoes on.)*

SALLY. Listen, thanks for the dress.

BEA. *(Crossing to the front door.)* Don't mention it. And I'll send Annie over Friday. Don't thank me twice. It would break your mouth.

SALLY. I won't open the door.

BEA. *(Opening the door, turning, smirking.)* I've got a key. *(SHE exits.)*

SALLY. *(Turns to David.)* That's some aunt you've got there. *(Crossing to him.)* Can you believe this? *(Rubbing her hand over her mouth to obscure the word.)* … I'm forty years old and I have a "date?" Come here. Be my date.

(SHE takes DAVID by the hand and leads him to the couch. HE acquiesces but keeps his eyes on the TV screen. SALLY sits down next to him, crosses her legs coquettishly and starts to flirt.)

SALLY. So, you're John. Pardon me for saying so, but I expected an older man. I'm fascinated by wallpaper. It's so sexy.

(DAVID looks at her and laughs, not understanding the point of it, but amused by his mother's obvious enjoyment. SALLY enjoys his enjoyment.)

SALLY. Oh, you like that one, huh? How about this? *(Again, the "dating act.")* Bea has told me so much about you. For once, she told the truth.

(DAVID howls at that.)

SALLY. Yeah? You like that?

(SHE starts to laugh with him. Suddenly, DAVID stops laughing. HE looks past her to the TV set as if she doesn't exist.)

SALLY. That's it? The joke's over? Come on, we're having a good time here. Forget the movie. Tell me a joke … *(Slowly her demeanor changes, SHE darkens, saddens.)* … Kids are always telling jokes. You know the one about why did the moron tip toe past the medicine cabinet? So he wouldn't wake up the sleeping pills. Tell me that one. Or the one where the moron threw the clock out the window so he could see time fly? Tell me a moron joke, David. Of all the people in the world, you ought to know a few moron jokes. Tell me one. What about the one where the moron took hay to bed with him so he could feed his nightmares? Tell me that one. Come on, David, tell me a joke …

(The LIGHTS dim.)

Scene 4

Sunday afternoon. The apartment is empty. SALLY
unlocks the front door and enters. Behind her, in the hall
is JOHN NICKLAUS. SHE stands in the doorway,
blocking his entrance to the apartment.

SALLY. Okay, I'm home and I didn't get mugged.
Thanks for the protection.
JOHN. (*Off.*) Can't I come in?
SALLY. I've got so much work to do ...
JOHN. (*Off.*) One quick drink?
SALLY. (*Beat.*) Okay.

(SHE steps aside and JOHN enters. HE's a pleasant
looking man with a ready smile and a desire to please.
HE wears a handsome sports jacket and tries to hide his
nervousness with Sally.)

SALLY. Be it ever so humble, there's no hovel like
home.
JOHN. It's nice.
SALLY. Try to hide your enthusiasm. (*Calls off.*)
Justine?
JOHN. I mean it. It's lived in.
SALLY. So's the Women's House of Detention. (*Off.*)
Hey, Justine, we're back.
JOHN. (*Picking up a note from the coffee table.*) "Dear
Aunt Sal, I took David to the park. Justy."

(There's a sense of relief in SALLY but SHE hides it from him.)

SALLY. So, what'd you want to drink? Harmless or poison?

JOHN. After all those Bloody Marys, why stop now?

SALLY. Okay. One lousy gin and flat tonic coming up.

(SHE goes to the kitchen. JOHN walks around the room looking it over.)

SALLY. *(Off.)* It's too quiet in here.

JOHN. I was just looking around.

SALLY. *(Off.)* Yeah, that's what I was afraid of. Had a tetanus shot lately?

JOHN. I meant it when I said it's nice. This apartment is about living, not showing off.

SALLY. *(Off.)* Yeah, we're distinctly downwardly mobile around here.

JOHN. You and Bea are very different.

SALLY. *(Entering with their drinks.)* I should warn you. I'm the only one allowed to trash her.

JOHN. I wasn't going to trash her.

SALLY. You weren't going to make a crack about that Sutton Place brothel she lives in?

JOHN. You haven't seen my apartment.

SALLY. Have you been architecturally digested, too?

JOHN. My wife's hobby is ... was interior decorating.

(An awkward pause at the mention of his wife.)

SALLY. I've run out of small talk. You wanna watch *E.T.*?

JOHN. Am I doing something wrong?

SALLY. You're doing just fine. It's me. I haven't been in a social situation with a man other than my dentist since they wrote the 1812 Overture. I'm out of practice.

JOHN. Me, too.

SALLY. Not you. You were great at brunch. You didn't shut up for a minute. I mean that as a compliment. (*Beat; looking for something to say.*) So, how long has your wife been dead? (*Off his reaction of surprise.*) Sorry, that was a little rough. I'm not good at this, you know? Give me a super who doesn't want to fix the sink and I'm as eloquent as a banshee. But plunk me down in front of a man in a sports jacket and tie and I'm a mute. So, if you want to get out of here, I'll understand.

JOHN. I don't want to get out of here.

SALLY. What are you, a masochist?

JOHN. You're funny. You make me laugh.

SALLY. Yeah?

JOHN. As a matter of fact, you're probably one of the wittiest women I've ever met. You may have noticed, I'm not particularly witty myself. But I'm smart. Did Bea tell you I'm thinking of opening a third store? In a recession? That's how well I'm doing.

SALLY. What are you, applying for something?

JOHN. (*Laughs.*) You see what I mean? That's witty. I like that. (*Beat.*) I think I've made a big enough fool of myself now. I think I'll shut up.

(*SALLY chuckles to herself, looking at him, shaking her head.*)

JOHN. (*Pleased.*) Do I make you laugh?

SALLY. No.

JOHN. I think I do. I like that, too.

SALLY. (*Despite herself, the flattery is getting to her.*) Don't get too full of yourself, buster. How's the drink?

JOHN. The tonic is flat.

SALLY. (*Putting him in his place.*) I know.

JOHN. Would you like to have dinner Friday night?

SALLY. Why? You need a laugh?

JOHN. I always need a laugh.

(*The front door opens. JUSTINE, a pretty girl in her late teens enters with DAVID. JOHN does not see them. HE has put down his drink and is preparing for his first sight of David, of whom he has heard a great deal.*)

JUSTINE. Sorry we're late. I couldn't get him out of the penguin house at the zoo.

SALLY. Yeah, he thinks they're Munchkins.

JOHN. (*Turns around, smiling.*) Hi, Justine.

JUSTINE. Hi, John.

(*JOHN's smile fades as HE sees David and the full impact of his illness. SALLY is watching John. As usual, her resentment of anyone staring at David clicks into place. SHE speaks with an edge to her voice, a phony casualness. SHE will not allow herself to show any embarrassment.*)

SALLY. John, this is my son. The one you heard so much about. David, this is John. (*A beat of silence.*) He's speechless. I guess he didn't expect you to be so handsome.

JOHN. I'm sorry, I …

SALLY. Don't sweat it. Lots of people are surprised at how handsome he is. Take your jacket off, David.

(*JUSTINE goes to help him. SALLY speaks with an edge.*)

SALLY. He can do it himself.

JUSTINE. (*As DAVID struggles awkwardly out of his jacket.*) You have any soda?

SALLY. As long as you don't require bubbles.

(*JUSTINE exits into the kitchen. DAVID completes taking off his jacket. There's a growing embarrassment between SALLY and JOHN.*
DAVID drops the jacket on the floor and hurries to the TV set.)

SALLY. (*Picking up his jacket.*) Hold your horses, kiddo. (*Joining him, selecting a video.*) How about Pinocchio? You haven't seen that in a couple of days. (*SHE sets up the tape as DAVID makes noises of happy anticipation.*) No sound and no intro. (*SHE turns to JOHN, who's been standing there awkwardly.*) He'll be fine till the boys turn into donkeys. That hits a little too close to home for him.

(*JOHN reacts to her apparent cruelty.*)

SALLY. So, where were we? Oh, yeah. You were talking about Friday night ...

JOHN. Yeah. Oh, damn. Can I call you about Friday? There's a possibility ...

SALLY. (*Cutting him off, matching his uncomfortable smile with her own defiant one.*) Of course. Don't sweat it. Listen, give Justy a lift back to the safe side of town, would you? I really have to get that manuscript finished. (*Calling off.*) Justy, you got a lift back to Oz if you move it.

JUSTINE. (*Off.*) Coming!

JOHN. Can I finish my drink?

SALLY. What for? It's not going to grow bubbles. Really, I got so much work to do.

JOHN. Alright.

(*HE puts the drink down as JUSTINE enters.*)

JUSTINE. Bye, Aunt Sal.

SALLY. Bye, kiddo. (*With a touch of resentment to John.*) Bye, kiddo.

JOHN. I'll call you.

SALLY. (*Exposing his lie, she thinks.*) You don't have my number.

JOHN. Of course I do. You think Bea would let me leave her house without it?

(*THEY exit. SALLY watches them go. Then SHE turns and crosses to David.*)

SALLY. What is it with people? Why can't they see how beautiful you are? (*SHE stares at David dreamily.*) Phil?

PHILLIP. (*Off. In the past.*) What?

SALLY. (*In the past, too.*) Come here and look at our son.

PHILLIP. (*Entering.*) Don't you see enough of him all day? You'll stare the skin off him.

SALLY. He's so pretty. Who would think to look at him that he's not like every other five year old? Getting into mischief, answering back, throwing a tantrum at the check-out counter because he wants gum ...

PHILLIP. I'm going to bed.

SALLY. I don't want you to go to bed. I want you to talk.

PHILLIP. Sally, it's late.

SALLY. Talk to me.

PHILLIP. What'd you want to talk about?

SALLY. Come here. Stand here with me and look at our beautiful son.

PHILLIP. Sally ...

SALLY. He is beautiful. No matter how short-circuited his neurological system is. Come look.

PHILLIP. (*Begrudgingly joins her.*) Yes, he's beautiful.

SALLY. He has your mother's nose. The one good thing about her and he got it. You got your father's nose.

PHILLIP. I also got his dick. That's two strikes against the old man.

SALLY. I like your dick.

PHILLIP. Thanks.

SALLY. A lot.

PHILLIP. I'm not in the mood for sex, Sally.

SALLY. Who asked you?

PHILLIP. Whenever you talk about body parts, that's where the conversation is going.

SALLY. Is it such a bad place for it to go?

PHILLIP. I'm just not in the mood.

SALLY. When're you going to be in the mood?

PHILLIP. You want to make an appointment?

SALLY. I wouldn't mind. At least then I'd have something to look forward to. Where have you been lately, Phil?

PHILLIP. Where have *I* been? Right here. Try looking at someone besides your son once in a while.

SALLY. *My* son? Boy, that says it all, doesn't it?

PHILLIP. That's not what I meant.

SALLY. (*Bitterly.*) *I do the best I can.*

PHILLIP. Yeah? Prove it.

SALLY. And how do I do that?

PHILLIP. Leave the kids with Bea for a weekend. Let's go to a hotel. (*SHE stiffens.*) Come on, you want me so bad? Come with me.

SALLY. You know I can't leave David.

PHILLIP. (*Beat, ruefully.*) Well, that says it all, doesn't it? (*HE turns to exit up right.*)

SALLY. You getting it somewhere else?

PHILLIP. (*Stops, turns, advances on her.*) No, I'm not getting it somewhere else. I'm not getting it. And you know what? I don't give a shit! I don't miss it. You know what I miss? I miss coming home and arguing about politics and whether or not we should get slip covers made for the couch and how much money we should spend and whether or not you cheated in Monopoly. I miss forcing down one of your terrible new recipes and seeing my daughter get giddy over nothing! I miss laughter! That's what I miss, not getting laid!

SALLY. (*Touched.*) I'm sorry.

PHILLIP. Sure, you're always sorry.

SALLY. (*Crossing to him.*) I'm always sorry because I'm always doing things I should be sorry for. Ask Bea. I was a rotten kid and now I'm a rotten grown up. But I love you. I even love your nose.

PHILLIP. Someday ...

SALLY. (*Putting her hand over this mouth.*) Someday nothing. You can't scare me. You love me too much to leave me. You're here for the duration.

(*THEY embrace, sadly.*
The LIGHTS dim.)

Scene 5

Late Friday night. The room is empty. The PHONE rings.
In a moment, JUSTINE enters from the kitchen with a
half-made sandwich and gets it.

JUSTINE. Hello? ... Hi, Ma ... No, they're not back yet. (*An idea comes to her, SHE smiles.*) Uh, they're not due back for another hour anyway. I'll see you later ... I gotta put David to bed ... I gotta go. Bye.

(*SHE hangs up, snickers to herself, goes back into the*
kitchen. The sound of a KEY in the front door lock.
JOHN and SALLY enter.)

SALLY. (*Calling out.*) Hello? The governor called. Your pardon came through.

JUSTINE. (*Entering.*) Hi. David went to bed about ten minutes ago.

SALLY. Yeah? How'd you manage that?

JUSTINE. We watched public television. (*Indicating a vase of red roses on the coffee table.*) Where'd you get these?

SALLY. (*Nodding toward John.*) Prince Charming showed up with them. He also offered to wallpaper the room, but I don't think I want to fuck with the decor. (*Catching herself, pointing at Justine.*) You didn't hear that.

JUSTINE. How was dinner?

JOHN. Sensational.

SALLY. Nouvelle something-or-other. You know, one still-born broccoli spear and one pigeon foot in a puddle of cream of mushroom soup.

JOHN. You said you liked it.

SALLY. I did. That's my version of a rave.

JOHN. (*To Justine.*) You want a lift home?

JUSTINE. No, I want a favor. From you both.

SALLY. What?

JUSTINE. I need to go somewhere for about an hour. I need you to say I was here.

SALLY. Sure. Nothing easier. Just do me a favor before you go?

JUSTINE. What?

SALLY. Take the knife out of my back that your mother's going to put there when she finds out I lied to her.

JUSTINE. Sally ...

SALLY. That's *Aunt* Sally to you, kiddo. As in your mother's sister. The one who tells her everything. Add the one who takes over kicking you in the ass when her foot's tired. Who's the boy?

JUSTINE. It's not like that.

SALLY. Then what's it like?

JUSTINE. (*Beat.*) That.

SALLY. Honey, you're the one who turned out good. Keep it that way, will you? These are dangerous times we live in. You've got to be careful ...

JUSTINE. Aunt Sally, I don't need a condom to *talk* to him.

SALLY. (*To John.*) Listen to the mouth on this kid. (*To Justine.*) Who do you take after?

JUSTINE. Are you kidding?

SALLY. (*Sighs, kisses Justine on the cheek and gets a few bills from her purse.*) In thirty minutes I'm calling your mother to have her ask you where you put my dictionary. And you'd better be there to answer. Thirty minutes.

(*SHE hands JUSTINE the bills. JUSTINE hurries to her coat.*)

JUSTINE. Mom's so unfair about him, just because he's an actor.

SALLY. An actor? Twenty minutes and not a second longer!

JUSTINE. (*Hurrying out.*) Bye, John. Bye, Sally.

SALLY. If they find my body floating in the East River, Bea did it. So, now that we've abetted the delinquency of a minor, you want another bad gin and tonic or a cup of rancid coffee?

JOHN. Neither. I should get home.

SALLY. Why? You been bad? Or have I?

JOHN. I have a full day tomorrow.

SALLY. Oh. Okay, hit the road.

JOHN. I had a great evening.

SALLY. (*Disappointed.*) Yeah, me too. Short and sweet.

JOHN. I'll call you.

SALLY. Okay.

JOHN. (*Getting his coat.*) It really was a terrific date.

SALLY. (*Unable to stop herself.*) Yeah? Is that why it took you three days to remember you asked me on it? (*Off his reaction of discomfiture.*) Who said that? (*SHE slaps her own cheek.*)

JOHN. Sally …

SALLY. No, come on, no excuses necessary. I shouldn't have said that. It comes from talking to David all day. I forget that other people don't have his tolerance for rudeness. Forget I said a word. Really. You mentioned the possibility of a date on Sunday, you called to confirm on Wednesday, you showed up on Friday. Emily Post lies quiet in her grave.

JOHN. Sally …

SALLY. (*Preventing him from going on.*) No, I mean, what more could anybody ask? Except why didn't you confirm on Sunday? Because you saw David?

JOHN. No. I mean, I wasn't really prepared for David. I suppose he did stop me in my tracks. But that's not why I didn't ask you out. That was because of something you did.

SALLY. What?

JOHN. You made fun of David. At least I thought you did. Then I spoke to Bea and she explained how sometimes, when you sound like you're being cruel, you're just making jokes to cover how uptight you feel. It doesn't mean anything. So I called you.

SALLY. You discussed my so-called sense of humor with my sister behind my back?

JOHN. Don't get mad.

SALLY. You are one presumptuous wallpaper hanger, you know that?

JOHN. I don't hang it. I sell it. Except to you. I give it to you. Any kind you want. (*Trying to wheedle her good will.*) Silk-screened, hand-painted, flocked ... Am I tempting you?

SALLY. (*Warming despite herself.*) You're nauseating me.

JOHN. That's a start. How about I take you *and David* out for dinner Tuesday night?

SALLY. David? In a restaurant? You are a masochist.

JOHN. I know a nice place in Chinatown.

SALLY. (*Still begrudging but won over.*) Come here. I'll cook.

JOHN. Yeah? That'd be wonderful.

SALLY. That's what you think.

(*Beat. JOHN leans in and kisses Sally briefly on the lips. HE breaks away, embarrassed. SALLY, however, is not embarrassed. SHE is interested.*)

SALLY. I lied about the tonic. I got a new bottle.

JOHN. I can't. Tuesday.

SALLY. At seven. Bring something that goes with lousy pot roast.

(JOHN exits quickly. SALLY crosses to the door and locks it. Beat.)

SALLY. *(Calling out to the bedroom.)* You have everything?

(PHILIP enters carrying a suitcase.)

PHILLIP. I think so.

SALLY. Your hair dryer?

PHILLIP. Sally, we're separating. You're not supposed to help me pack.

SALLY. I'm sorry. I don't know the etiquette of divorce.

PHILLIP. It's not a divorce. It's a separation.

SALLY. Does that mean you'll be home for dinner? I'm making liver. Maybe you'd better skip tonight. Tomorrow I'll make pot roast. Should we expect you?

PHILLIP. You make things more difficult than they already are.

SALLY. That's my talent. Give me something difficult and I'll make it impossible.

PHILLIP. This isn't your fault.

SALLY. Of course not. I'm perfect. Everybody runs away when things get too good. You're still sure there's nobody else?

PHILLIP. I've told you a thousand times.

SALLY. So make it a thousand and one.

PHILLIP. There's nobody else.

SALLY. Good. I'll make noodles with the pot roast.

PHILLIP. Just give me a while.

SALLY. Take all the time you want. I'm not going anywhere.

(SUSAN runs into the room and to Phillip. HE embraces her. THEY part, HE picks up his suitcase.)

SALLY. Susan, go to bed. I want to talk to Daddy.

SUSAN. I want to stay.

SALLY. Go to bed! *Now!* *(SUSAN reluctantly leaves the room.)* One more thing before you go?

PHILLIP. What?

SALLY. I want you to tell me the truth, because if you don't, you won't come back. It's easier to stay away than to come back to a lie.

PHILLIP. *(Putting down the suitcase.)* What do you want to know?

SALLY. I want to know about the woman you're going to. The one who's waiting for you.

PHILLIP. *(Pause. HE gives in.)* She isn't a woman. She's a girl from the office. She's nothing.

SALLY. Then why are you going to her?

PHILLIP. Because I don't know where else to go.

SALLY. You could stay here.

PHILLIP. I can't.

SALLY. Why not?

PHILLIP. I just can't do it anymore! *(An old pain.)* I can't face one more father in the playground. I can't watch him look at David and then at his own boy. I can't bear the relief on his face. Or the pain in the eyes of the women when David falls down and hurts himself. Or my own mother's voice when she asks after her grandson. The sudden self-conscious gentleness in her voice. I can't bear it.

SALLY. You think I can?

PHILLIP. Yes, I think you can. I think you can do anything.

SALLY. Listen, before you turn me into some kind of saint and I lose you for good, I want you to know that not one day goes by that I don't blame David for what isn't his fault. Not one day when I don't think "What did I do to deserve this?" But I dress him and feed him and clean him and sometimes I hate him. I have this fantasy. One day he'll wake up healed and tell me he knew what I did for him all along. He knew every time I wiped his ass or sat around watching some goddamn movie with him. You see, that's the worst of it. I need to be thanked and he can't thank me. (*Beat.*) But I do what I have to. So, if you come back, it's to someone who knows how hard it is to do what you have to do and who understands that sometimes you have to go away and rest. So go away and rest. And when you've rested, make up your mind.

PHILLIP. (*Stares at Sally, moved. Then HE picks up his suitcase and crosses to the door, stops, turns.*) I love you.

SALLY. Of course you do.

(*HE leaves. SHE stands there for a moment staring at the door. DAVID hurries on in his pajamas and heads for the TV set.*
SALLY follows him. Cradles him in her arms.
SUSAN enters and hesitates, watching them.)

SALLY. (*To David.*) It's just you and me, David. Just you and me.

(*SUSAN has heard it and is unable to speak.*
The LIGHTS slowly dim.)

End of ACT I

ACT II

Scene 1

Tuesday evening. The desk has been cleared and reset as a dining table. The remnants of a candlelight dinner for two sit on it. SALLY and JOHN are on the couch, sipping wine.

Downstage DAVID sits watching a movie with no audio. His dinner tray is on the floor next to him.

SALLY. You want some more wine?

JOHN. Please.

SALLY. I don't have any.

JOHN. Then why'd you ask?

SALLY. To be polite. Should I run out and get you some? There's an all night liquor store a few blocks away, next to a crack house and a welfare hotel. I'll put on my good pearls and go.

JOHN. (*Laughing.*) You talked me out of it.

SALLY. Good.

JOHN. That was great pot roast.

SALLY. Thanks.

(Suddenly DAVID becomes upset. HE points at the TV and yelps in great distress.)

SALLY. What? (*SHE crosses to him and looks at the set.*) Big deal, the movie's over. (*SHE spins back the tape.*) Why don't you hit the sack, kiddo?

(*DAVID whines in protest.*)

SALLY. I mean it, David. I want you to go to bed. (*HE wails.*) Stop it! Now! (*HE calms somewhat. To John.*) Would you mind?
JOHN. Of course not.
SALLY. (*To David; reaching for another cassette.*) No sound, no intro and no more bullshit, you hear me?
JOHN. (*As SHE sets it up.*) Why don't you teach him to do it himself? That way he won't have to bother you.
SALLY. Yeah, I'm going to do that. Right after I teach him how to use a computer.
JOHN. (*Getting up, crossing to David.*) Wait a minute. It's not that hard.

(*JOHN gets between Sally and the machine. SHE steps back, folding her arms. HE removes the tape and holds it up to David.*)

JOHN. You see this side of the cassette, David? This side goes in here. See? It slides right in.

(*HE slides the cassette into the VCR slowly several times while DAVID looks on, mesmerized.*)

SALLY. Hey, Mr. Wizard, it took me a month to learn how to use that thing. What d'you expect from him?
JOHN. Patience. Rome wasn't built in a day.

SALLY. (*A sigh.*) What d'you take in your coffee?
JOHN. A little milk.

(*SALLY exits into the kitchen. DAVID points at the set
and makes a noise of impatience.*)

JOHN. (*To David.*) First we've got to press this button.
Here, you do it.

(*JOHN takes David's finger and presses the VCR button
with it. The VCR goes on with audio.*)

JOHN. Now, off.

(*JOHN turns it off. DAVID squeals.*)

JOHN. Press it again, David. Come on.
SALLY. (*Off.*) He doesn't know what you want him to
do. Just put the movie on.
JOHN. He's never going to know unless I show him.
(*To David.*) That's right. Press the button.

(*DAVID becomes more upset. JOHN releases his hand.*)

JOHN. Press it again. You can do it. *Press the button.*

(*DAVID wails and SALLY hurries in.*)

SALLY. Just put the movie on, will you?!
JOHN. (*Beat, surprised by her vehemence.*) Sorry.

(HE pushes the play button and the movie starts. DAVID smiles, he's won.)

SALLY. (*Beat.*) No, I'm the one who's sorry. (*SHE crosses to the set and turns off the volume. SHE strokes David briefly.*) It's just that people who don't know David think if they talk loud he'll turn normal. He won't. You can wake him up in the middle of the night and he still won't understand. He's not kidding around.

JOHN. I know. But I think I can teach him. I'd like to try.

SALLY. Just take it easy, okay?

JOHN. Okay.

SALLY. So, you want Sara Lee pound cake with Haagen Daz butter pecan ice cream or Pillsbury microwave brownies?

JOHN. Neither. I'd better get going.

SALLY. *Again?*

JOHN. (*Ignoring her sarcasm.*) I was up at the crack of dawn.

SALLY. Oh. You want to take your coffee with you? You could drink it in the cab. Or were you going to run all the way home?

JOHN. You mad?

SALLY. Me? Naw.

JOHN. Good. (*HE kisses her cheek and crosses to get his coat.*)

SALLY. A little disappointed, that's all. Don't get me wrong, I'm not that kind of girl, but I thought after a while we'd bundle David off to bed and fool around a little.

JOHN. (*Weakly.*) It's late.

SALLY. Yeah, it must be going on ten. Maybe you don't find me attractive in that way, huh? No sweat. I don't find me attractive in that way, either.

JOHN. It isn't that.

SALLY. No? You're not gay, are you? (*SHE smiles. Beat. The smile fades.*) Are you?

JOHN. (*With difficulty.*) No, I'm not gay. I'm married. My wife died a year ago and even though she's gone, she's still my wife. That didn't die. When I left you the other night and went home, I half expected her to be there. To ask me where I'd been and who with. I felt like I had cheated on her. I feel the same way now.

SALLY. That's why you run out of here?

JOHN. Yeah. Can you understand that?

SALLY. (*Crossing to him.*) Understand it? I can top it. I'm cheating on my husband. He thinks he's married to someone else, the government thinks he's married to someone else, but I know the truth. He's still my husband. I've just had more time to get used to the idea of cheating than you have. (*SHE touches his cheek affectionately.*) Now get out of here before I hit on you again and embarrass you.

(*As JOHN crosses to the front door, BEA enters from the kitchen, in the past, unseen. SHE carries a box of crackers and a drink.*)

BEA. Zabar's was a zoo. Ever since the gentiles discovered lox, you can't get in the place.

JOHN. How about I order in for us Friday night at my place?

SALLY. I'm a fool for shrimp and lobster sauce. Go.
I've got a pound cake and a pan of brownies to eat.

(HE smiles and leaves the apartment.)

BEA. These crackers are stale.
SALLY. *(Turning, in the past now.)* You want me to
zap you something?
BEA. When's the last time you cooked?
SALLY. I don't know. What's-his-name was still here.
BEA. His name's Phil.
SALLY. He left five months ago, so I haven't cooked
in five months. It's one of the many benefits of not having
him around.
BEA. *(Beat, uncomfortable with this.)* He called me last
night.
SALLY. Yeah?
BEA. He signed a lease on an apartment in the Village.
SALLY. Good. Every village should have an idiot.
BEA. There's a place there for special ed kids that's
supposed to be good. Only you have to live in the district
to be eligible.
SALLY. So?
BEA. So, David's father lives in the district!
SALLY. I'm not putting David in any home, Bea.
BEA. It's not a home. It's a school. Besides, Phil said
he'd pick him up every Tuesday afternoon and keep him
overnight. You know what that means?
SALLY. It means one idiot would take care of another.
BEA. It means you could have a couple of days off.
Come on, he's his father. Let him do some of the work.
SALLY. Forget it.

BEA. For crying-out-loud, why?! You're denying yourself to punish Phil.

SALLY. He walked out on his own kid! David is as much his fault as mine. I'm not going to let him ease his conscience by taking him out for pizza once a week.

BEA. (*Beat.*) "Fault?" David isn't anyone's *fault*. One out of ten kids is born impaired. He's one of the one out of ten, that's all.

SALLY. Fine. It's nobody's fault.

BEA. Well, it isn't!

SALLY. (*Bitterly.*) God, that's so nice! It must be wonderful to live in a world that's so nice. No fault accidents, no fault divorces, no fault murders ... It's so damn *nice*.

BEA. Why are you attacking me?

SALLY. Because it's bullshit! They don't have a clue what caused David to be born with scrambled eggs instead of a brain, but *you* know it wasn't me? I wish *I* knew that, Bea, I wish I knew it was the fluoride in the water or the asbestos in the ceiling or the lead in the fucking paint. I wish to Christ I wasn't on the list of suspects for the joint I smoked when I was carrying him or the wine I was so sure couldn't hurt him or the sex in the eighth month or some genetic fuck up in my chromosomes!

BEA. Stop that! You'll drive yourself crazy thinking things like that! Stop that right now!

SALLY. (*Begrudgingly.*) Alright, I stopped.

BEA. It's Ma's fault.

SALLY. What's Ma's fault?

BEA. She always blamed you so now you blame you. Come here, I want to hold you in my arms.

SALLY. Don't be ridiculous.

BEA. (*Crossing to her with open arms.*) Let me hold you.

SALLY. (*Starting to laugh, backing up.*) Get away from me, you moron.

BEA. Let me hold you!

SALLY. Oh, Christ. (*Begrudgingly, SALLY permits BEA to embrace and hold her. Beat.*) "The Children's Hour." Shirley MacLaine and Audrey Hepburn.

(*BEA starts to laugh and releases her.*)

BEA. (*Forcing herself to stop laughing.*) You don't always have to make jokes. I know how much you hurt. I know how much you want Phil back.

SALLY. What?! Bea, listen to me carefully. See if you recognize any of these words. I don't want him back. I wouldn't take him back if you presented him to me on a silver platter with an apple up his ass! Am I getting through to you?

BEA. (*Not believing a word.*) Yeah, yeah.

SALLY. Would you please stop being the authority on my feelings?!

BEA. Alright, I'm sorry. I just think somebody besides you should bear some of the burden. What if, God forbid…

SALLY. Say it. I won't drop dead because you said it.

BEA. Well?

SALLY. I don't want to talk about it.

BEA. It wouldn't kill him to take David overnight.

SALLY. Sure. Him and his girlfriend. I wouldn't trust that bleached tramp to watch my kid for two minutes.

BEA. He'd be with his father.

SALLY. (*Sarcastically.*) What's second prize.

BEA. How do you know she's bleached? You've seen her!

SALLY. Yeah. I dropped Susan off at his office a couple of months ago. I could tell which one she was.

BEA. How?

SALLY. She didn't look up from her typewriter once. She just sat there, her face red and blotchy and pounded the keys. She's a little fat thing. She wore a high-collared dress to cover her big tits and hardly any makeup. Just a little baby blue eye shadow, like some sweet little virgin. And her hair was dyed a very nice color, if you happen to be a golden hamster. She looked like she should have been carrying a tray of beer steins at an Octoberfest. I had quite a good look at her while we waited for Phil. After five minutes, she started to sweat. I hoped she'd drip into her electric typewriter and set herself on fire, but no luck. She just sat there, hunting and pecking like crazy. She looked like a kid at a piano recital with her mother in the audience with a gun. And then she gave this miniature sneeze, like a bug, and she dabbed at her nose with a little ladylike hanky and I said "Bless you" and she said "Thank you" but her eyes never left the typewriter. And I knew it was her. I hoped Phil wouldn't show up for an hour so when he did his girlfriend would be sitting there, her rodent hair matted to the side of her head by sweat, two baby blue rivers pouring down her fat cheeks, her heart pounding like a set of bongos beneath her stretched out dress. But he showed up and I left. But not before I said something to her.

BEA. (*Enjoying this.*) What?

SALLY. Just "Have a nice day." Out of all the things I could have said, to let her know I knew who she was, to

make her spit sweat like a pig on a rotisserie, all that came
out was "Have a nice day." I ask you, am I a saint or what?

BEA. (*Getting up, crossing to kitchen.*) A saint? You're
an idiot. If it were my Stephen, she would have been
wearing her typewriter as an I.U.D.

(*DAVID leans into the VCR and presses a button. The tape
ejects. HE wails, bringing SALLY back into the
present. SHE crosses to him.*)

SALLY. If you're going to press the button, the
movie's going to stop. (*Starting it again.*) A little
knowledge is a dangerous thing, huh? Alright, hands off.

(*SHE crosses to the desk and starts to clear the dishes.
DAVID leans forward and presses the eject button, once
again, the movie stops, HE wails. SALLY crosses and
starts it again.*)

SALLY. Thanks a lot, John. Thanks a lot.

(*The LIGHTS dim.*)

Scene 2

A few afternoons later.
*GLADYS JOHNSON is sitting on the couch. DAVID is
sitting in his chair watching TV.*

GLADYS. (*Calling off to Sally.*) He's in San Diego living with some woman. And he still doesn't have a job and I can't get any money out of him.

SALLY. (*Entering from the kitchen with two cups of tea.*) Sometimes I think the continent is tilted the way all the men keep sliding to California. My ex is in L.A. (*SHE hands GLADYS a cup.*)

GLADYS. Thanks, this is nice.

SALLY. It's not so nice. I used the same tea bag for both cups. (*SALLY crosses to the TV and turns off the sound.*) So, how's your son?

GLADYS. His sister's got it now.

SALLY. Ain't it the way.

GLADYS. Shall we talk about David now, Sally, or do you want to stall some more?

SALLY. I'd prefer to stall if it's all the same to you.

GLADYS. David's older now. He might be ready for what a program could do for him.

SALLY. Or *to* him.

GLADYS. Come on, give a little, will you? I *know* your son can be helped. And that's not department bullshit. I've seen kids worse off than him ...

SALLY. There *is* nobody worse off than him!

GLADYS. (*Beat, gently.*) You mean there's nobody worse off than *you*, don't you?

SALLY. (*Beat.*) Fuck you, lady.

GLADYS. Sally, I've seen kids who can't even watch TV because their eyes don't work together! I've seen kids who can't sit in a chair ...

SALLY. So don't complain about no shoes. Think of the guy with no feet. Hallelujah.

GLADYS. (*Losing it, getting angry.*) *Lady,* whether you like it or not, whether you believe me or not, whether you trust me or not, your son is going into a program because that's the law and that's what's going to happen. Just as sure as the law *won't* force my children's father to get a job and support them, it *will* put your son in a program!

(*Silence. A deadlock.*)

SALLY. (*In control.*) What do you suggest?

GLADYS. There's a small facility on Thirty-fifth Street. They take a limited number of kids ...

SALLY. Great. If he gets scared, he can run over to Macy's and do a little shopping.

GLADYS. Why assume he's going to get scared? They're just teenagers, like him.

SALLY. (*Turning to look at David as HE stares at the TV screen.*) Like him? Does he look like a teenager to you?

GLADYS. Yes. What's he look like to you?

SALLY. A little boy. (*Quickly to cover the moment of softness.*) Tell me about the place.

GLADYS. They're heavy into vocational guidance. The object is to make the kids self-sufficient. Or as close as they can get. It's set up like a co-ed dorm, two kids to each room ...

SALLY. (*Surprised.*) They sleep there?

GLADYS. Yeah.

SALLY. When do they go home?

GLADYS. On weekends. Parents pick them up on Saturday morning and return them Sunday night. (*Beat.*) Most parents like it that way.

SALLY. There are other programs, aren't there? Less Nazi oriented?

GLADYS. Yes, but I strongly recommend this one.

SALLY. (*A look of determination comes across Sally's face. SHE hides it from Gladys.*) Give me some time?

GLADYS. I already did.

SALLY. I need more.

GLADYS. How much?

SALLY. A couple of weeks.

GLADYS. Sally ...

SALLY. Two weeks? What's that? Harass somebody else for a while.

GLADYS. (*An edge of resentment in her voice.*) Thanks for that.

SALLY. Gladys, have a heart! Don't get mad at me! You're not asking to take my kid for a walk around the block! You're asking to take him away!

(*A moment of silence in which GLADYS relents.*)

GLADYS. Two weeks.

(*GLADYS heads for the front door. Before she reaches it, the door opens and BEA enters in the past, unseen. SHE passes Gladys.*)

BEA. I had Mexican food for lunch. Water! Water!

(BEA enters the kitchen and SALLY follows GLADYS to the front door.)

SALLY. Sorry if I was rude. My charm school burned down before I graduated.

GLADYS. No problem. *(Turning to Sally.)* You know, just because this is my job doesn't necessarily mean it's wrong.

SALLY. Doesn't mean it's right, either.

GLADYS. *(Almost laughing.)* You're a piece of work.

SALLY. Thanks. I love you, too.

(GLADYS exits as BEA enters from the kitchen.)

BEA. Why don't you keep a pitcher of water in the fridge so it's cold?

SALLY. *(Turning into the past.)* Bea, there's no Mexican restaurant in this neighborhood. What're you doing? Coming all the way crosstown just to annoy me?

BEA. Would it be too much to expect to hear "It's nice to see you" once in a while?

SALLY. It is nice to see you. *Once in a while.*

BEA. Where's Susan?

SALLY. At school.

BEA. Good. *(To David.)* Hello, sweetheart.

SALLY. Why good?

BEA. *(Grimly.)* Phil's getting married.

SALLY. *(Beat, stunned.)* Do me a favor. Don't say anything else. I'm not through dealing with that one yet. *(SHE takes a deep breath and sits.)* How do you know?

BEA. He called me.

SALLY. Who's he marrying? Somebody who dropped by to sell him Girl Scout cookies?

BEA. She writes for *Time* Magazine. She's forty-six.

SALLY. Oh. (*Beat.*) Hey, David, you've got a stepmother. Thanks for rushing over with the good news.

BEA. Are you alright?

SALLY. Do I look alright?

BEA. You look like somebody punched you in the stomach. I suppose I did. I'm sorry.

SALLY. Who cares if he gets married? I didn't think he left me to become a priest. I hope they'll both be very happy. (*Beat.*) With frequent intervals of not-so-happy.

BEA. Why don't I call Stephen? He'll take us out to dinner. Some place nice.

SALLY. I'm not hungry.

BEA. You'll be hungry later.

SALLY. I don't think so.

BEA. Then get the sitter and let's go shopping. I'll buy you something.

SALLY. Bea, I don't want a nice dinner and I don't want you to buy me anything. Go home.

BEA. Sally ...

SALLY. Please. Just go home.

BEA. Call me later?

SALLY. Tomorrow. Go.

(*BEA hugs an unwilling SALLY and crosses to the front door. Stops.*)

SALLY. I'm alright, I promise.

(BEA exits. SALLY crosses to David, still sitting on her emotions.)

SALLY. Your father's getting married so you can drop any thoughts of his coming back to us. That's over. She's forty-six. Even older than me. I didn't think anybody was older than me. I bet she's got kids. Maybe a boy around your age. It's going to cost him plenty. He'll have to send him to college. He didn't know when he was well off. *(SHE crosses to her desk and gets a cigarette. Lights it.)* So much for till death do us part, huh, kiddo? They ought to rephrase that. Till inconvenience do us part. Till trouble do us part. Till need do us part. *(SHE grinds out a cigarette.)* Who cares? Who the hell cares? *(SHE goes to the closet and gets her coat and DAVID's jacket.)* We can do just fine without him! Come on, kiddo. We're going to the zoo. Let's look at some monkeys besides ourselves. I'll buy you a balloon if you promise not to sulk after you break it. Let's go. Everybody in the elevator. *(SHE turns off the TV and DAVID whines loudly.)* Let's go, David!

(HE pulls his arm out of her grasp, determined to remain there and watch his movie. SALLY struggles to get him to his feet.)

SALLY. We're not going to sit here, David! We're going out and we're going to have fun! Move it! *(SALLY fairly drags David out of the apartment after her. SHE speaks with an edge of hysteria.)* We got each other, we got the Big Apple at our door, what the hell else does anybody need?!

(SALLY and DAVID exit. SHE slams the door after her.
The LIGHTS dim.)

Scene 3

Evening. Several days later.
SALLY and JOHN lie on the couch, SALLY in his arms.
  THEY're only partially dressed, having made love for
  the first time.

JOHN. So, when are you going to let me paper this
place?

SALLY. (*A sigh.*) It would make the furniture look
shabby.

JOHN. Let me buy you some new furniture.

SALLY. (*Sitting up.*) What is with you? You got laid.
I didn't give you a kidney. You don't owe me anything.
(*SHE crosses to the desk for a cigarette.*)

JOHN. Yes, I do. You're like ... the sun shinning your
light on me. I owe you.

SALLY. I've got news for you. Women like sex, too.
Besides, I was the one who pushed *you* into it.

JOHN. See? I owe you even more.

SALLY. Do yourself a favor. Play a little hard to get,
will you?

JOHN. Okay. (*Beat.*) I can't. Not with you. Can I give
you a compliment without your yelling at me?

SALLY. Make it quick.

JOHN. You're a wonderful lover. You're not afraid to
enjoy yourself.

SALLY. Thank you and shut up.

JOHN. Most women …

SALLY. (*Mock, shouted at God.*) Why doesn't this man understand English?

JOHN. Sorry. (*A moment's pause.*) Can I talk now?

SALLY. As long as it isn't about me.

JOHN. It isn't. It's about Big Sur. Have you ever been there?

SALLY. If it takes more than two hours to get to, I haven't been.

JOHN. Bea told me your daughter is getting married in L.A. I thought I could meed you there after the wedding and we could drive up the coast …

SALLY. Sounds wonderful, only I'm not going to the wedding.

JOHN. Why not?

SALLY. Among other things, I wasn't invited.

JOHN. You're kidding.

SALLY. Yeah. Some joke, huh?

SUSAN. (*Off.*) God damn it (*SUSAN enters from up right, at age sixteen. SHE's upset over something.*)

SALLY. (*Turning to her, entering the past.*) Watch the mouth, kiddo.

SUSAN. Why can't I go?!

SALLY. Susan, you're not talking to a moron. This is your mother. I know what kind of girl Sandra is. And you're not spending a weekend at her house without her parents there.

SUSAN. Nothing will happen to me!

SALLY. You're damn right nothing will happen to you. You won't be there.

SUSAN. There won't even be boys there!

SALLY. Please. If Sandra's there, there'll be boys. Wherever she is, it's rutting season.

SUSAN. Well, what am I supposed to do here?!

SALLY. What you always do.

SUSAN. (*With more than a little bitterness.*) Watch you take care of David.

SALLY. (*Getting angry.*) Watch the mouth.

SUSAN. It's all you ever do.

SALLY. He needs it! He's not like you. He can't take care of himself.

SUSAN. Then let me take care of myself. Let me go!

SALLY. (*Beat, softening.*) Come on, Susan, let's skip this fight. What'd you say? I'll owe you one. Tomorrow you can be a real pain in the ass but today, let's lighten up. I'll take you and David out to dinner, okay? Some decent food for a change?

SUSAN. Did it ever occur to you that I don't want to be with you and *him*?

SALLY. (*Beat.*) Yeah, it's occurred to me. Did it ever occur to you that you're mad at me all the time? Give me a break, kid.

SUSAN. Just let me go, okay?

SALLY. No.

SUSAN. Christ, I'm like a fucking prisoner ...

SALLY. (*Losing it, a warning.*) I don't want to hear that language out of you.

SUSAN. Jo said she thought it would be fun.

SALLY. (*Getting angry.*) I don't care what your father's wife said.

SUSAN. I'm not a child!

SALLY. (*Putting her foot down.*) You're *my* child. And you're not going anywhere.

SUSAN. You know where I really want to go? I want to go live with Daddy and Jo!

SALLY. (*Said lightly, not meaning it.*) So go, who's stopping you?

SUSAN. You don't think I would?

SALLY. I think you should. Go to Jo. What kind of woman has a man's name? She sounds like somebody on a sitcom. Good! You'll make it a sitcom. The new wife, the daughter comes to live with them, you'll all laugh a lot and you'll learn something every half hour.

SUSAN. (*Daring her.*) You don't think I'd go?

SALLY. You think she'd take you? You think you're such a prize package?

(*THEY freeze for a moment, horns firmly locked. Then SUSAN bolts for the front door and leaves. SALLY calls after her.*)

SALLY. You're not going anywhere!

(*The sound of elevator DOOR opening and closing. SALLY, filled with regret, comes back to the present and John.*)

SALLY. Even if I were invited, I wouldn't go.

JOHN. Why not?

SALLY. Susan and I have beaten up on each other enough. Better to let it lie.

JOHN. Better than what?

SALLY. Than the way it used to be. You may find it hard to believe, but I don't have a winning phone personality. I mean to say, "I miss you" and it comes out

"Why don't you ever call me?" I think I'm about to say, "Honey, don't do that, it could hurt you" and suddenly I'm yelling. You're not supposed to yell in L.A. You're supposed to lie back and sip your orange juice and if your kid does something bad, you have a barbecue and it goes away. But I live in New York and I happen to be her mother so I thought it was up to me to pull her back to the real world. That doesn't make you very popular. Pretty soon your kid has a chip on her shoulder the size of the Rock of Gibraltar and so do you. So you keep your mouth shut and you pray that the guy she's marrying because she's knocked up isn't one of California's serial killers and you remind yourself that you weren't that close to your mother and your daughter's not that close to you and in the end, when we've all had our turn at raising and alienating our kids it won't matter in the least, so why get upset about it when you're bathed in afterglow with a man who thinks the sun rises and sets on your ass? (*Beat*.) Glad you asked?

JOHN. Is Bea going to the wedding?

SALLY. No.

JOHN. How about we ask her to watch David for a few days and I take you to Key West?

SALLY. What for?

JOHN. It's called a vacation. You know, sunburns, bad drinks with umbrellas in them, sand in all your cracks ...

SALLY. Sounds great but I can't.

JOHN. Why not?

SALLY. I just can't.

JOHN. Everybody's entitled to a vacation. Even you. (*Crossing to the phone*.) I'll call Bea and arrange it.

SALLY. (*With an edge.*) Hey, Mr. Take Charge, I said I can't go, alright?

JOHN. *Why?*

SALLY. (*Beat, unsure of whether or not to tell him.*) Because David and I are moving in a few days.

JOHN. Moving?! Where?!

SALLY. To a little town in Connecticut with a church and a steeple and a couple of antique shops. (*Beat.*) To Fort Lee, New Jersey.

JOHN. (*Growing upset.*) Why?

SALLY. I have my reasons.

JOHN. Why didn't you tell me?

SALLY. I'm telling you.

(*A moment of silence. JOHN is stunned and the hurt is coming.*)

JOHN. Will I see you?

SALLY. You got bus fare? You'll see me.

(*The LIGHTS dim.*)

Scene 4

The next morning.

DAVID and JOHN are sitting in front of the VCR. They've obviously been involved in a lesson for some time. DAVID is dressed in pajamas. JOHN in a t-shirt and pants, no shoes or socks.

JOHN. (*Holding up a video tape.*) ... Okay, David, now remember this is the side that goes into the machine. The one with the wiggley edge. Okay, now you see it, now you don't.

Okay, you put it in.

That's right! Good boy. Let's try it again.

Okay, let's see you do it again.

Great! That's great. Now, you remember which is the play button?

No, that was rewind. This one is play. See?

Shh, let's not wake your mother. Okay, enough for one morning. You deserve the movie.

SALLY. I'm up. Let the games begin. Morning, what's-your-name. O.J., coming up.

JOHN. Just a minute, we've got something to show you.

SALLY. Yeah? You made breakfast?

JOHN. Better.

(*HE presses eject and takes the tape out of the VCR. DAVID whines.*)

JOHN. Patience. First you have to show Mother how smart you are. (*Puts the tape behind his back, turns it and hands it to David.*) Do your stuff.

(*DAVID takes the tape, examines it, wiggles the edge and puts it into the VCR.*)

JOHN. See? He knows how to insert the tape.

SALLY. (*Pleased but not overjoyed.*) Oh, that's wonderful. You're both wonderful. (*With a smile to John.*)

And for your reward, fresh squeezed orange juice from a
carton! (*SHE goes into the kitchen.*)
　　JOHN. (*To David.*) Now, remember the play button?

(*DAVID attempts to hit the wrong button again.*)

　　JOHN. Nope, the one next to it. This one. See?

(*DAVID frets.*)

　　JOHN. Hey, you're half way there.

(*HE turns the movie on. SALLY enters with the carton of
　　orange juice and one glass.*)

　　JOHN. Here, I'll give it to him.
　　SALLY. That's okay. I'll do it. (*SHE crosses to
David.*) I'm sorry. I forgot your glass.
　　JOHN. No problem.

(*JOHN exits into the kitchen. SALLY hands the glass of
　　juice to David.*)

　　SALLY. Take it slow, David. For once, let's not have a
spill. (*DAVID starts to drink but lifts the glass too high.*)
Be careful … (*HE starts to spill the juice.*) David! Damn it!
(*Calling off.*) John, get me a dish towel, will you? (*Taking
the glass.*) Oh, look at you …

(*JOHN hurries out of the kitchen with the cloth. SALLY
　　hold up her hand for it.*)

SALLY. Throw it.

JOHN. I'll clean him up.

SALLY. (*Insistent.*) Just hand it over, will you?

JOHN. (*Disturbed by her urgency.*) Whatever you say.

SALLY. (*Cleaning David and the floor.*) I'm going to feed you in the bath tub from now on … (*Looking under the chair; coming up with old, dried pasta.*) What is this? When did we eat this?

JOHN. (*Comes up behind David and puts his arm on the boy's shoulder affectionately.*) Don't worry about it, David. Mothers are always griping about spills. When I was a kid, my sister and I had "the great beet fight." You should have seen the expression on my mother's face when she came into the room …

(SALLY has gotten up from the floor and watches John and David as DAVID looks up at John and smiles. Her own face tightens.)

JOHN. … There were beets everywhere. On the walls…

SALLY. David, go to your room. I'll be right there to get you dressed. *Go.*

(DAVID obeys. JOHN looks at Sally, disturbed. When David is out of the room:)

JOHN. Why did you do that?

SALLY. Do what?

JOHN. Every time I get close to David, you break us up. Why?

SALLY. You're crazy. I do not.

JOHN. Yes, you do. This morning, the other night with the VCR ...

SALLY. He's my kid. I'm taking care of him, that's all.

JOHN. I don't think that's all. I think you won't let me get close to either of you. Like last night ...

SALLY. I won't let you get close to me? We did it twice. I hardly call that not letting you get close to me.

JOHN. That's not what I mean. I mean when you mentioned you were moving. In passing. Like I wasn't important enough for you to confide in.

SALLY. What did you want? An engraved change-of-address announcement? I'll call Tiffanys.

JOHN. Don't do that.

SALLY. *Now* what did I do?

JOHN. Don't mock me.

SALLY. Oh, Jesus, I wasn't mocking you. You know my mouth ...

JOHN. There's somebody *listening* to what comes out of that mouth. Don't use it as a weapon.

SALLY. Boy, they put out once, they think they own you. I'm sorry. I couldn't tell you because ... (*With difficulty.*) I'm breaking the law. I'm running away. If I stay here, they'll take David away from me.

JOHN. What?! And you kept that to yourself?!

SALLY. It's not your problem.

JOHN. Of course it's my problem.

SALLY. Look, you're a great guy. You dress nice, you laugh at my jokes, you're terrific in bed, but this particular problem is mine alone. I've been dealing with it for seventeen years. I think I know what I'm doing.

JOHN. In other words, fuck off.

SALLY. That sounds like something *I'd* say.

JOHN. You did say it.

SALLY. John, have a heart, I'm fighting for my kid's life here. I don't have time to tip-toe around, worrying about other people's feelings.

JOHN. Why not? I fought for my wife's life. *I* had time.

SALLY. It's different. I'm his mother.

JOHN. Why is that different? You think you love your son more than I loved my wife?

SALLY. He needs me! You know the way he is!

JOHN. (*Spoken half to himself.*) I know the way you let him be.

SALLY. What?

JOHN. Never mind. Just let me get dressed.

(*HE exits into the bedroom. SHE stares after him. After a beat—*)

SALLY. Great. Go. That'll solve everything.

(*PHIL enters from the bedroom. Both HE and SALLY are in the past, in the midst of another fight.*)

PHILLIP. Let me take a walk, huh? Anything I say now I'll regret. You'll regret it too, I promise you. (*HE heads for the front door.*)

SALLY. What is that, a threat?

PHILLIP. No. It's an observation. Based on a hundred fights and a thousand regrets.

SALLY. (*Beat, urgently.*) Don't go.

(As SHE says this, JOHN enters, dressing, from the bedroom. HE hears the line as if it were addressed to him. From now on, SALLY will move between past and present, caught between the two. PHILLIP comes back into the room.)

JOHN. It's better if I do. I don't want to say anything to hurt you.

SALLY. *(To John.)* You've got something to say, say it. Haven't you heard? I've got elephant's skin.

JOHN. Alright. It was very hard for me to put my wife in one part of my heart and let you into the other. And I don't think you'll ever do that with David.

SALLY. *(Bitterly.)* There's a little difference here. David isn't dead. No matter what some people wish.

PHILLIP. *(Having heard the gist of Sally's last remark.)* What are you, crazy?! I don't wish him dead! I'm his father! I love him!

SALLY. *(To Phillip.)* Yeah, from *afar*.

PHILLIP. That *is* love. What *you* do—breathing in the air as it comes out of his lungs—is lunacy! It's not good for him!

SALLY. *(Icily.)* I think I know a little better than you what's good for David.

JOHN. Do you?

SALLY. What the hell does that mean?

JOHN. It means I have to teach him to use the VCR while you're asleep, so you won't stop me.

SALLY. Big deal. It's not going to change his life.

JOHN. Don't diminish what I did or what he did!

SALLY. What d'you want from me?

PHILLIP. I want a wife! Not just a mother for my kid.

SALLY. Then trying being a father to your kid! Try helping him.

JOHN. You won't let me! You're so damn sure you know what he can do and what he can't do, you don't let him do anything!

SALLY. Listen, I don't need you to tell me how to live.

PHILLIP. Yeah, you don't need anybody.

SALLY. That's right, I'm not a charity case.

JOHN. Everybody is a charity case who needs someone! I need someone! I don't want to be alone anymore!

SALLY. And I don't want my kid to be alone!

PHILLIP. How could he be alone? He wears you like a second skin. Nobody else can get near him. Not ever me!

SALLY. (*To Phillip.*) You want to get closer to David, get closer.

JOHN. How?!

SALLY. (*To both.*) Stop it! I'm fighting for David's life! I don't have time for all these goddamn feelings!

JOHN. That's the second time you said that. You're not fighting for his life. You're fighting to *control* his life.

PHILLIP. You use him. Don't you see that?

SALLY. (*To both.*) That's a terrible thing to say! I've sacrificed *everything* for him!

PHILLIP. No. You've sacrificed every*one* for him!

(*A freezing of the THREE of them. Then, tight and hurt, SALLY speaks.*)

SALLY. You said you wanted to leave. So leave.

*(Beat. BOTH MEN leave the apartment, one after the other.
SALLY stands there watching them go.
DAVID enters from his bedroom carrying a shirt, still
dressed in his pajama bottoms. HE comes up behind
Sally and pushes the shirt at her, startling her for SHE
didn't realize he was there.)*

SALLY. What?! (*Seeing him.*) Not now, David. (*HE
pushes the shirt at her again.*) Leave me alone.

*(DAVID stares at her, shocked by her indifference. His
attitude changes. Sulking, HE tries to put the shirt on
himself as SALLY crosses away and lights a cigarette.
HE fails to get the shirt on and throws it on the floor
angrily. HE hurries to the TV set. Slowly and with
great deliberation, HE presses the eject button on the
VCR and removes the old tape. HE throws it on the
floor.
SALLY turns and sees him do this. SHE watches as he
goes on.
DAVID selects a new tape and puts it into the VCR. With
a look of defiance at his mother, HE presses the
appropriate button and the movie begins. HE smiles
triumphantly.
SALLY is stunned. SHE goes to him. SHE presses the
eject button and removes the tape.)*

SALLY. (*Tenuous, not daring to believe it.*) Do it
again, honey.

*(HE stares at her, smiles and puts in a new tape, turning it
on.)*

SALLY. (*After a half laugh half cry, SHE ejects that tape, too.*) Again. Again.

(*Now it's a game that DAVID enjoys. HE puts another tape into the VCR and turns it on. HE looks to her for approval. Her reaction is mixed: happiness, sadness, confusion.*)

SALLY. David, go I'll be right there to get you dressed.

(*DAVID understands and runs off happily. SHE stands there, staring at the TV screen.*
The DOORBELL rings.)

SALLY. It's open.
BEA. You leave your door open in New York City. What's the matter, you tired of living? (*SALLY not answering.*) At the risk of repeating myself, what is the matter?
SALLY. John just left. We had a fight.
BEA. So, couples fight. Even Stephen and I did before he adjusted to my always being right. Here, drown you sorrows in a Danish.
SALLY. Bea, tell me something. (*Thoughtfully.*) Am I a bad person?
BEA. What're you talking about? You're the best.
SALLY. Just tell me the truth, alright?
BEA. Alright. What happened?
SALLY. David can work the VCR.
BEA. What?

SALLY. In a million years, would you have believed that he could work a VCR?

BEA. I guess not.

SALLY. We had the goddamn machine in the house for three years and he never touched it. A few weeks with John and he's an expert. You remember how long it took you to teach me how to use it?

BEA. Are we talking about how smart David is or how dumb you are?

SALLY. John said I don't let David do anything. Maybe he's right. If he can work a VCR, who knows what he can do? Who knows what he can *be*?

BEA. What he can be? Honey, David *is* what he can be. He's impaired.

SALLY. That's just a word. Did *I* decide what it meant? Did I make him that way?

BEA. Stop it. You're not that important. *God* made him that way.

SALLY. Maybe there are two Gods, Bea. The one that cooked his brains and the one that made sure they stayed that way.

BEA. What do you think you did that's so terrible? You had an afflicted child, you took care of him, that's all. Nobody could have been a more devoted mother.

SALLY. Really? You think Susan would agree with you? (*BEA appears uncomfortable with that.*) And what about Phil? Was I a devoted wife, too? (*BEA says nothing.*) You said you'd tell the truth, remember?

BEA. You did the best you could. That's all anybody can do.

SALLY. And how *was* my best, Bea.

(BEA turns away, unwilling to answer.)

SALLY. If you thought I was doing something wrong, why didn't you tell me? You're my sister.

BEA. *(Admitting she knew all along.)* Would it have done any good? Did you ever once listen to anybody but yourself?

SALLY. No, I suppose not.

BEA. *(Crosses to her, puts her hands on Sally's shoulders. Gently.)* In your whole life, you never had anybody in your corner. Not even as a kid, I was the pretty one, remember?

SALLY. *(With a rueful smile.)* You weren't so pretty.

BEA. Compared to you I was.

(THEY both enjoy this.)

BEA. So I kept my mouth shut and I loved you. Was that so terrible?

SALLY. I don't know.

BEA. *(Beat, then with emotion.)* You did the best you could do!

SALLY. Go home. Your daughter's seeing that actor behind your back. See? I can keep my mouth shut, too.

(BEA embraces Sally silently. Then breaks away and heads for the front door.
SHE stops, turns.)

BEA. We can't be blamed for what happens to us. If they broke our legs, we can't be blamed for limping. If they wouldn't hold us, we can't be blamed for not letting

go. So you didn't let go of David, so what? You think he
would have been president if not for you? He wouldn't have
been president. He wouldn't have come close. Alright, I'll
go home now and beat up my daughter. (*SHE opens the
door, stops.*) Let me tell you something else. You don't
have to be so hard on yourself all the time. It doesn't make
you more important that your punishment is always the
worst. (*With that, BEA exits and closes the door after her.*)

Scene 5

Morning. A week later.
The room is empty. The front DOORBELL rings. SALLY
*   enters from the bedroom and gets it. SHE admits BEA.*

BEA. You haven't said more than two words to me on
the phone all week. What's going on?
SALLY. I've been busy.
BEA. Doing what?
SALLY. Selecting my fall wardrobe.
BEA. Well, you better go put some of it on. We're
going to lunch at Tavern on the Green. And then on to
Bloomingdale's. We'll drop David off at my place. Justine
will watch him. She's not leaving the apartment till she's
thirty. Incidentally, she sends you her love.
SALLY. Bea, I've had two hours sleep. I'm not up to
all this forced gaiety.
BEA. Tough.

SALLY. Can I at least have a cigarette before you burst into song? (*Crossing for it.*) It's going to cost you a bundle.

BEA. I'm not buying lunch. John is. We're meeting him.

SALLY. Bea, I can't. Not today.

BEA. You have to. John's going to ask you something while I pretend I have to go to the ladies room.

SALLY. What?

BEA. He's going to ask you to have an understanding with him.

SALLY. What kind of understanding?

BEA. (*Happily.*) The kind of understanding that could lead to *dinner* at the Tavern. For three hundred people.

SALLY. Don't dye your shoes, Bea.

BEA. (*Suspiciously.*) What does that mean?

SALLY. It means I don't know if I'm interested.

BEA. What d'you mean you don't know if you're interested?!

SALLY. I don't know how I feel about the man.

BEA. Of course you do! You like him!

SALLY. But what if I don't love him?

BEA. *Love*? What does love have to do with anything? Who thought you would *love* him?

SALLY. Didn't you? Isn't that what you hoped for?

BEA. *Love*? Of course not. You still love Phil. I know that. I hoped for companionship. Comfort. *Help*. He's a rich man, Sally. He can take you out of this crummy apartment! Out of this crummy life! You could have a woman to come in and watch David. Vacations in Europe. You could hold your head up and walk the aisles of Bloomingdale's like a normal person!

SALLY. (*Beat.*) Did you hear what you just said?

BEA. I don't care what I said! He's crazy about you. There's nothing he wouldn't give you.

SALLY. Why do I have to marry him? Why don't I just forge his name on a check?

BEA. (*Angrily.*) Don't make jokes and ruin your life!

SALLY. I don't believe what I'm hearing. Weren't you in love with Stephen when you married him?

BEA. I was twenty-four years old! I was *entitled* to be in love!

SALLY. And I'm not? When did I lose that entitlement, Bea? At what age did I become a charity case? When David was born? Did his illness make *me* unworthy? Or was it when Phil left and I became that most pitiful of all things, *a woman alone*?!

BEA. That's not what I'm saying.

SALLY. Then what are you saying?! Bea, no matter what harm I've done to anyone, I've done more harm to myself. I won't do this final act of self degradation! I won't settle. I won't be ground into a victim or dismissed as a loser! I will not settle!

BEA. I'm not asking you to.

SALLY. Yes, you are. Of course you are.

BEA. I'm asking you to save yourself!

SALLY. No, you're not. You're demanding it. Why?!

BEA. Because I'm exhausted from worrying about you! I've been savaged by guilt! I don't have the energy to care about you anymore!

SALLY. (*Gently, no trace of resentment.*) But you don't have to. You never did. I never asked for it. I never wanted it.

(A long, tired pause during which the SISTERS look at each other sadly.)

BEA. Tell me something. Why do the people who *don't* fuck up their lives always feel guilty over those who do? Why do they always pay the price for those who refuse to pay it for themselves?

SALLY. I don't know.

BEA. God, I resent you.

SALLY. *(Indicating the VCR.)* I know. I've got the gifts to show for it.

BEA. I hate you.

SALLY. And I love you.

BEA. *(On the verge of tears, softening despite herself.)* Well, I hate you.

(THEY embrace.
The DOORBELL rings.)

SALLY. Ours is not a simple relationship.

BEA. Who says simple is good? You know the parts I meant and the parts I didn't.

SALLY. Of course.

(SALLY opens the door. GLADYS enters.)

GLADYS. Hi.

SALLY. Hi. Bea, this is Gladys Johnson. She's a friend of mine. And David's.

GLADYS. Hello.

SALLY. My sister. She was just leaving.

BEA. Yeah. I'm going shopping. I'm going to buy myself something fabulous. I need it.

(BEA leaves. GLADYS turns to face SALLY who is suddenly upset.)

GLADYS. Did I interrupt something?
SALLY. Just our usual best two out of three falls. (*Suddenly with desperation.*) Gladys, I'm sorry. I can't do this. I'm not ready for it.
GLADYS. You're never going to be ready. You've just got to do it.

(SALLY considers this and decides Gladys is right. SHE slowly exits into the bedroom. GLADYS walks around the room. SALLY enters with DAVID. His appearance is quite different. HE wears a clean white shirt and a tie and slacks, not jeans. His hair has been combed and he looks quite handsome.)

GLADYS. Hiya, handsome.

(DAVID hurries past her to the TV set.)

SALLY. Not today, kiddo.
GLADYS. (*To David.*) Remember me? Gladys?

(DAVID starts to insert a cassette into the VCR.)

GLADYS. No movie today, David. Today we got an adventure. You and I are hopping on the 1-0-4 bus and heading downtown.

(HE presses play and the movie starts. SALLY starts to him.)

GLADYS. We'll have a lot more fun than just sitting around watching the tube.

SALLY. Enough of that, David.

(SALLY turns off the TV set. DAVID has a flash of rage, yells.)

GLADYS. *(Reaches for his hands.)* You know what I tell my kids when they plant themselves in front of the TV?

(DAVID slaps her hands away, hard.)

GLADYS. Honey, that's not allowed.

SALLY. Gladys, I can't do this!

GLADYS. You promised. I gave you two weeks, now you've got to give me two weeks.

SALLY. God.

GLADYS. Does David have a jacket, Sally? *(SALLY looks on helplessly.)* His jacket?

SALLY. Yeah. I'll get it.

(SALLY crosses to the closet for the jacket as DAVID struggles against GLADYS who is obviously used to this.)

GLADYS. You know what, David? We're going to go see this great place today. They've got a pool and a ping pong table ...

(HE tries to fight her off while SALLY hurries to them with his jacket.)

GLADYS. David, I want you to calm down. Nobody's going to hurt you. Come on ...

(SALLY tries to get his jacket on him, but DAVID will not permit it. HE hurries away from Sally and Gladys, across the room, fretting and whining.
GLADYS goes after him. HE tries to hit her away.)

SALLY. Cut it out, David ... cut it out!

(DAVID wails at the top of his lungs and falls to the floor in a hysterical tantrum. SALLY hurries to him, puts her arms around him to calm him.)

SALLY. David, stop this. Stop it right now. (*DAVID looks at Gladys and wails.*) Let me talk to him.
GLADYS. Sally.
SALLY. Please! Let me talk to him! Go have a cup of coffee.

(GLADYS gives in and exits into the kitchen. SALLY cradles David in her arms, still sitting on the floor.)

SALLY. Come on, sweetheart. Nothing bad is happening. Shh. Come on, calm down. That's a good boy.

Calm down. (*HE starts to whimper. His struggling subsides.*) We've got to talk, sweetheart. I've got to talk and you've got to do your best to listen. (*HE continues to calm.*) Try to listen, honeybunch. (*SHE strokes him, HE sighs and falls silent.*) I want you to go with Gladys. I know, I promised you wouldn't have to. But I was wrong. Things stink around here. They have for a long time. I just got a whiff of the stench. It's not your fault, sweetheart. It's mine. (*SHE strains for the truth.*) You see, in my whole life, I was never special. I was never pretty enough, or smart enough or talented enough to be anything but ordinary. And then you came along and you were the way you were. And I was the only one who could handle you. Do you have any idea how special that can make a person feel? You know you're a piece of work just like me. I could get you up in the morning and get you dressed and fed and happy. I could make you happy. So I kept it that way. For me. Not for you. I kept us here watching movies. And I stayed special. And you stayed calm. But you know something? Being calm isn't all there is. There's a whole world out there, David. Even for you. Hey, you can work a VCR! So I want you to go with Gladys. Let's see what other tricks you've got up your sleeve. Because the truth is, I may not be special at all, but you sure as hell are!

(*THEY get up off the floor and SALLY hugs David.*)

SALLY. Alright, my speech is over. Help my kid?

(*DAVID takes Sally's hand and swings it happily. GLADYS comes out of the kitchen and crosses to*

David's other side. SHE takes his hand. DAVID drops
Sally's hand and swings Gladys's.
SALLY gets David's jacket and hands it to him. GLADYS
attempts to help him on with it.)

SALLY. He can do it himself.

(GLADYS backs off. DAVID puts the jacket on while
SALLY looks on triumphantly. Then GLADYS takes
DAVID by the hand and leads him to the front door.)

GLADYS. Oh, I know what I forgot to tell you.
They've got a crafts room there. Now, I don't know if
you're into leather, but one of the guys made a belt there
that was out of this world. He sold it to the girlfriend of
one of the counselors for fifteen dollars. I could've killed
her that she got there before me ...

(At the front door, DAVID turns and looks across the stage
at Sally. SHE turns and looks back at him as if across a
great abyss. SHE smiles encouragingly at him.
Hold.
GLADYS leads him off and closes the door.
SALLY hurries to the landing, as if to call David back.
SHE changes her mind and locks the door.
SHE looks down into the room and opens the curtains.
SHE looks at the club chair in which David has spent so
many years.
SHE moves it to face the couch, balancing its counterpart.
It is now part of the seating arrangement and no longer
apart.
SHE looks out over the room, feeling her aloneness.
SHE goes to the phone and dials.)

SALLY. Is Susan Goodman there? Tell her ... tell her it's her Avon representative. No, tell her it's her mother. (*The LIGHTS dim.*)

THE END

COSTUME PLOT

SALLY
I,1,2
Green long-sleeved pullover top
Jeans
Green overcoat
Black loafers
Brown purse
Black camisole

I,3
Same jeans
Salmon sweatshirt
Change to:
Burgundy rayon dress
Black shoes

I,4
Add earrings
Taupe sweater coat

I,5
Jeans
Maroon silk blouse
Patchwork blazer

II,1
Orange tucked blouse
Black leggings
Black loafers

II,2
Same leggings
Forest green sweater
Same loafers

II,3
Pink chenille robe
Bra and undies

II,4
Add grey socks

II,5
Blue sweater
Jeans
Grey socks

BEA
I,1
2-pc wool, plaid suit
Purple silk charmeuse blouse
Black pumps
Nude pantyhose
Black leather purse
Diamond ring
Wedding band
Fuchsia wool wrap
Two Gold chains
Gold earrings
Gold watch

I,3
2-pc silk suit
Shoe, pantyhose, purse (repeat)
Gold earrings
Gold bangle bracelet
Rings (repeat)
Watch (repeat)
Gold and black wool shawl

II,1
2-pc. black and white print suit
Pantyhose (repeat)
Black with grey suede shoes
Rings (repeat)
Double strand of pearls
Pearl and silver earrings
Watch (repeat)

II,2
2-pc grey silk suit
Black and white polka dot blouse
Shoes (repeat black and suede)
Rings (repeat)
Earrings (repeat)
Suede purse
Silver broach

II,4
Green gabardine pants
Turtleneck sweater
Rings (repeat)
Watch (repeat)

Gold earrings

II,5
Dark ranch mink coat
Purple silk dress
Gold pumps
Pantyhose
Black purse w/gold chain
Fuchsia leather gloves
Rings (repeat)
Black mirrored triangle earrings
Multicolor print scarf
Watch (repeat)
Fur hat

DAVID
I,1
Navy and green striped knit shirt
Burgundy sweat pants
Converse, low-top sneakers
White socks
White cotton t-shirt, crew neck

I,2
Repeat I,1

I,3
Gold and navy striped t-shirt
Jeans
Repeat shoes, socks, t-shirt

I,4
Turquoise stripe shirt, yellow collar
Green pull-on pants
Blue hooded sweat shirt jacket
Repeat shoes, socks, t-shirt

I,5
Fishing print pajamas
Bare feet

II,1
Blue and red striped t-shirt
Repeat rest of costume

II,2
Same as II,1, add plaid shirt over t-shirt

II,4
Repeat pajamas
Button-front shirts (2, one for beginning of scene in green
   and white seersucker, one for end of scene in madras
   plaid)

II,5
Green and white striped shirt
Khaki trousers with cuff and pleats
Repeat sneakers, socks
Brown belt
Navy blue wool coat with knit collar

PHILLIP
(always in the past, usually in shades of grey)
I,1
2-pc double-breasted suit
White shirt with grey stripes
Black and white tie
Blue nubuck shoes, wing tips
Grey patterned socks
Black leather belt, silver buckle
Glasses
Black cotton trench coat
Silver wedding band
Silver watch

I,4
Pants front suit above
White t-shirt, crew neck
Socks, belt, glasses, wedding band, watch (repeat)

I,5
Black and white shirt
Black corduroy slacks
Black "Topsider" shoes
Belt, socks, wedding band, overcoat, watch (repeat)

II,4
Grey crew neck sweater
Grey jeans
Black belt
Shoes, socks, glasses, wedding band, watch (repeat)
Grey cotton jacket

JOHN
I,4
Brown/rust/green glen plaid sports jacket
Brown wool trousers
Brown leather belt
Burgundy print tie
Penny loafers
Brown socks
Wedding band
Watch

I,5
Brown and black tweed sports coat
Trousers (repeat)
Cream shirt w/small check
Burgundy knit tie
All weather taupe trench coat
Shoe, socks, belt, wedding band, watch (repeat)

II,1
Green cotton corduroy trousers
Shirt (repeat I,3)
Striped wool necktie
Sports jacket (repeat black and brown tweed)
Overcoat (repeat)
Brown lace up shoes
Green socks
Brown leather belt
Watch, wedding band (repeat)

II,3
Blue patterned boxer shorts

Athletic cut t-shirt

II,4
Gold knit cotton pullover shirt
Burgundy corduroy pants
Overcoat, socks, belt, watch, ring (repeat)
Loafers with tassels

II,5
Overcoat (carries over arm – repeat)
Green herringbone wool sports coat
Green, gold and red stripe tie
Cream cotton shirt
Shoes (repeat tasseled loafers)
Brown socks
Brown wool trousers (repeat)
Belt, watch, ring (repeat)

GLADYS
I,1
Trench coat, khaki
Dark forest green skirt
Navy and ochre tweed v-neck sweater
Navy cotton blouse
Briefcase
Brown leather flat shoes
Pantyhose
Gold watch w/brown leather band
Small gold hoop earrings

I,2
(repeat I,1, carrying coat)

II,2
Jacket, cotton
Navy rayon skirt
Teal silk blouse
Shoe, stockings, bag (repeat)
Watch, earrings (repeat)
Gold scarf around hair

II,5
Purple, mauve cotton jacket w/belt
Ochre cotton knit skirt
Navy blue blouse, turtleneck
Shoes, ankle boots
Pantyhose, bag, watch, earrings, head scarf (repeat)
Wool neck scarf, earth tone plaid w/fringe

SUSAN
(always in past)
I,1
White and grey striped sweater
Pale grey corduroy slacks
Grey "Keds" sneakers
White socks

I,2
White polka dot turtleneck blouse
Grey jeans
White sweatshirt
White "Keds" sneakers
White socks

I,5
2-pc pajamas, grey w/white eyelet and smocking
Bare feet

II,3
Grey thermal knit blouse
Black cotton knit skirt
Black suede shoes, flats
Vintage man's wool vest w/silver pins
White stretch headband
Silver wire earrings w/balls
Grey sheer opaque tights

JUSTINE
I,4
Forest green ribbed knit cotton tights
Floral dress (green, blue, gold, w/green yoke)
Mustard colored cotton sweatshirt jacket
Earrings
Bag: embroidered (India type import)
Ochre/gold cotton socks
Large watch w/black band

I,5
Green/purple plaid leggings
Purple and gold top
Shoes
Red and black tweed man's sports coat
Brightly colored earrings

PROPERTY PLOT

Top of Show Preset

<u>Desk and Filing Cabinet</u>
Phone
Picture of Susan
Picture of David
Ashtray w/sand
2 letters from Gladys
Empty cigarette pack
Lighter
Box of matches
Several manuscripts and books
Extra cigarettes in desk drawer
Phil's appointment book (buried US side)
Brown mug of water
Chair angled out
David's file (2 inches thick) top drawer filing cabinet
Trash can (DS side, grocery bag showing)

<u>Coffee Table</u>
Cheap bottle of wine (1/2 filled)
Empty wine glass
Ashtray w/sand and short, bent butts
Small ashtray with sand (SL side)
2 Lighters (on either side of ashtray)
Box of matches
Several magazines (messed up)
2 Xerox magazines buried SR and SL
Several newspapers (under table)
Small Kleenex package w/1 popped up

Sofa, End Tables & Console
7 Pillows (arranged as 3-2-2)
Blanket (on back of sofa, messed up)
Cigarette pack partially full (hidden in SR cushions)
Ashtray with sand (SL end table)
Kleenex box on SL of sofa
SL lamp angled over Kleenex box

David's Chair and Table
Table against "wall" touching TV
4 Toys (arranged SR of chair)
Wood blocks (DSR side of chair)

TV Cart
VCR empty
4 Video tapes (no jackets, under TV) labeled as Star Wars,
    ET, Pinocchio, and Wizard of Oz (Wizard on top of
    others)
Misc. video tapes (behind TV)
TV knob pulled out and turned to the left

Toy Box
Slinky
Pad of paper w/crayon stuck to it
Box of large crayons
Purple block bucket
Box of Kleenex
Roller coaster toy

USC Table Area
Magazines and scripts (2 stacks)

3 Board games
4 Chairs (SR chair turned out, center chairs together and
  pushed SL)
Curtains closed

<u>Closet</u>
Door closed
Empty

<u>Door</u>
Closed
Un-chained

KITCHEN

<u>Counter</u>
Ashtray with sand
Tray with: 2 red dishtowels, 2 spoons

<u>Top Shelf</u>
4 Gin glasses (set zig zagged)
Gin bottle (1/2 filled with water & loosen lid)
Justine's soda glass (SL side)

<u>Microwave</u>
2 Macaroni & cheese dinners (1 with fake food set SL side,
  1 with real macaroni set SR side [needs to be hot, set
  approx. 5 till curtain])

<u>Bottom Shelf</u>
Pack of cigarettes with lighter and box of matches
Brownie w/napkin

Plastic drop cloth

Fridge
Tonic bottle (1/2 filled w/ water and loosened lid)
4 Ice cubes (in egg tray)
2 Liter 7-Up bottle (1/2 filled with water)
Chair set in front of fridge

Offstage Right
3 Dresses on plastic hangers
Bills
Glass of milk
Suitcase
Cigarette pack (partially full)
Vase of roses
Justine's I,5 maroon coat
Note
Make-up bag
David's shirt
2 Black dishtowels
Carpet sweeper
Red dishtowel
Script w/pencil
Grey tray w/2 plates, 2 forks, 2 napkins, 2 coffee mugs
All Act II kitchen props

Offstage Left
Bag of groceries
Sally's keys
Sally's black clutch purse
Susan's tote bag
Gladys' briefcase and purse

Phil's briefcase
Zabars bag
Mail
Phil's keys
Justine's bookbag
Justine's keys
David's gym bag
Monopoly board (under table w/ 2 cars, money, 1 car on N.
   Carolina 1 on Kentucky Ave.)
Pack of cigarettes and lighter
Zabar's bag with 2 Danishes and papers
Puzzle (7 pieces loose)
David's shoes
Piece of pizza
Sally's wallet
Spoon
3 Video tapes (red, blue & yellow)
Plastic stacking blocks
Bottle of scotch
Dry macaroni pieces
Justine's I,4 tan coat
Susan's denim jacket and black purse
John's coat
David's grey coat
David's coat and hat

Other
Sally's purse w/money in side pocket and unzipped
Pair of dice